THE
WORLD'S
ONE THOUSAND
BEST POEMS

~

VOLUME FIVE

GUEST-KING

THE
WORLD'S
ONE THOUSAND
BEST POEMS

(IN TEN VOLUMES)

BERTON BRALEY

EDITOR-IN-CHIEF

VOLUME FIVE

GUEST-KING

(*Complete Index—Volume Ten*)

FUNK & WAGNALLS COMPANY

NEW YORK AND LONDON

TABLE OF CONTENTS

VOLUME V

	Page
GUEST, EDGAR	
Home	11
GUINEY, LOUISE IMOGEN	
The Wild Ride	13
GUITERMAN, ARTHUR	
Hills	14
Strictly Germ-Proof	15
HALLECK, FRITZ GREENE	
Marco Bozzaris	16
On the Death of Joseph Rodman Drake	19
HARRIS, JOEL CHANDLER	
My Honey, My Love	20
HARTE, BRET	
San Francisco	22
The Heathen Chinee	24
The Aged Stranger	26
Her Letter	27
HAWKER, ROBERT STEPHEN	
The Song of the Western Men	30
HAY, JOHN	
Jim Bludso	31
Little Breeches	33
HEBER, REGINALD	
Holy Holy, Holy	35
HEINE, HEINRICH	
Loreley	36
The Grenadiers	37
Du Bist Wie Eine Blume	38
Belshazzar	39

TABLE OF CONTENTS

	Page
HEMANS, FELICIA	
The Homes of England	41
The Landing of the Pilgrim Fathers	42
Casabianca	44
HENLEY, WILLIAM E.	
The Christian Slave	45
Song of the Sword	46
Invictus	51
Midsummer Days and Nights	52
HERBERT, GEORGE	
Discipline	53
HERRICK, ROBERT	
To the Virgins, To Make Much of Time	54
To Daffadills	55
The Night-Piece, To Julia	56
A Ternarie of Littles, upon a Pipkin of Jellie Sent To A Lady	57
Cherrie-Ripe	57
Delight In Disorder	58
Corinna's Going A Maying	58
Love Me Little, Love Me Long	61
Upon Julia's Clothes	61
Anacr(e)ontick Verse	61
The Pillar of Fame	62
To Fortune	62
HEYWOOD, THOMAS	
Pack, Clouds Away	63
HITOMARO	
On Parting from His Wife	63
HAFIZ	
From the Diwan of Hafiz	64
HO, CHANG CHI	
A World Apart	66
HOGDSON, RALPH	
Stupidity Street	67
Time, You Old Gipsy Man	67
HOGG, JAMES	
The Witch of Fife	68

TABLE OF CONTENTS

	Page
HOLMES, DANIEL HENRY JUNIOR	
Margery Daw	80
HOLMES, OLIVER WENDELL	
Old Ironsides	82
The Wonderful One-Hoss Shay	83
The Last Leaf	87
The Height of the Ridiculous	89
Contentment	90
The Comet	92
The Chambered Nautilus	95
HOMER	
Extracts from "The Iliad"	97
Extracts from "The Odyssey"	112
HOOD, THOMAS	
The Bridge of Sighs	116
The Song of the Shirt	119
Fair Ines	122
The Dream of Eugene Aram	124
Ruth	131
I Remember, I Remember	132
Gold	133
Faithless Nelly Gray	134
HOPE, LAURENCE	
Valgovind's Song In the Spring	136
Kashmiri Song	137
Less Than the Dust	138
HORACE	
To Chloris	139
To Pyrrha	140
Persicos Odi	141
Vitas Hinnuleo	141
HORNE, RICHARD HENGUIST	
Pelters of Pyramids	142
HOUSMAN, A. E.	
When I Was One and Twenty	143
Myself Again	144
With Rue My Heart Is Laden	144
Mithridates	144

TABLE OF CONTENTS

	Page
HOVEY, RICHARD	
The Sea Gipsy	147
Stein Song	148
Barney McGee	149
HOWE, JULIA WARD	
Battle Hymn of the Republic	152
HOWELLS, WILLIAM DEAN	
Heredity	154
HUGO, VICTOR	
To A Woman	154
The Djinns	155
Her Name	159
HUNT, LEIGH	
Abou Ben Adhem	161
Jenny Kissed Me	161
Jaffar	162
IBSEN, HENDRIK	
A Swan	163
Solveig's Song	164
The Petrel	164
INGALLS, JOHN JAMES	
Opportunity	165
INGELOW, JEAN	
The High ...... on the Coast of Lincolnshire	166
INGERSOLL, ROBERT G.	
Life Is A Narrow Vale	172
IRWIN, WALLACE	
From Romany To Rome	172
Song For A Cracked Voice	174
IRWIN, WILL	
Heroic Ballad, 1976	175
JOHNSON, SAMUEL	
One-And-Twenty	179
JONES, SIR WILLIAM	
What Constitutes A State?	180
JONSON, BEN	
Hear Me, O God!	181
Hymn To Diana	182

TABLE OF CONTENTS

	Page
JONSON, BEN (*Continued*)	
The Noble Nature	182
To Celia	183
JUDGE, JACK AND WILLIAMS, HARRY	
It's A Long, Long, Way To Tipperary	183
KAO SHIH	
Desolation	184
KEATS, JOHN	
A Thing Of Beauty	185
Ode To A Nightingale	186
Ode On A Grecian Urn	189
Sleep	192
A Hymn To Pan	192
On First Looking Into Chapman's Homer	194
The Mermaid Tavern	194
La Belle Dame Sans Merci	195
Ode To Autumn	197
The Eve Of St. Agnes	198
Bards of Passion And Of Mirth	190
KEMP, HARRY	
Thanks	211
The Conquerors	212
KENYON, THEDA	
Heredity	213
KEPPEL, CAROLINE	
Robin Adair	214
KEY, FRANCIS SCOTT	
The Star-Spangled Banner	216
KHAYYAM, OMAR	
The Rubaiyat of Omar Khayyam	218
KILMER, JOYCE	
Trees	237
KING, BEN	
The Pessimist	237
If I Can Be By Her	238
If I Should Die	240
The Cow Slips Away	240

THE
WORLD'S 1000 BEST POEMS

EDGAR GUEST

1881—

HOME

It takes a heap o' livin' in a house t' make it home,
A heap o' sun an' shadder, an' ye sometimes have
t'roam
Afore ye really 'preciate the things ye lef' behind,
An' hunger fer 'em somehow, with 'em allus on yer
mind.
It don't make any differunce how rich ye get t'be,
How much yer chairs an' tables cost, how great yer
luxury;
It ain't home t'ye, though it be the palace of a king,
Until somehow yer soul is sort o' wrapped round
everything.

Home ain't a place that gold can buy or get up in
a minute;
Afore it's home there's got t' be a heap o' livin'
in it;
Within the walls there's got t' be some babies born,
and then
Right there ye've got t' bring 'em up t' women good,
an' men;
And gradjerly, as time goes on, ye find ye wouldn't
part

With anything they ever used—they've grown into
    yer heart:
The old high chairs, the playthings, too, the little
    shoes they wore
Ye hoard; an' if ye could ye'd keep the thumbmarks
    on the door.

Ye've got t' weep t' make it home, ye've got t' sit
    an' sigh
An' watch beside a loved one's bed, an' know that
    Death is nigh;
An' in the stillness o' the night t' see Death's angel
    come,
An' close the eyes o' her that smiled, an' leave her
    sweet voice dumb.
Fer these are scenes that grip the heart, an' when yer
    tears are dried,
Ye find the home is dearer than it was, an' sanctified;
An' tuggin' at ye always are the pleasant memories
O' her that was an' is no more—ye can't escape from
    these.

Ye've got t' sing an' dance fer years, ye've got t'
    romp an' play,
An' learn t' love the things ye have by usin' 'em
    each day;
Even the roses 'round the porch must blossom year
    by year
Afore they 'come a part o' ye, suggestin' someone
    dear
Who used t' love 'em long ago, an' trained 'em jes'
    t' run
The way they do, so's they would get the early morn-
    in' sun;

Ye've got t' love each brick and stone from cellar
    up t' dome:
It takes a heap o' livin' in a house t' make it home.

LOUISE IMOGEN GUINEY
1861—

THE WILD RIDE

*I HEAR in my heart, I hear in its ominous pulses,
All day, the commotion of sinewy, mane-tossing
    horses;
All night, from their cells, the importunate tramp-
    ing and neighing.*

Cowards and laggards fall back; but alert to the
    saddle,
Straight, grim, and abreast, vault our weather-worn,
    galloping legion,
With a stirrup-cup each to the one gracious woman
    that loves him.

The road is through dolor and dread, over crags and
    morasses;
There are shapes by the way, there are things that
    appal or entice us:
What odds? We are knights, and our souls are but
    bent on the riding!

*I hear in my heart, I hear in its ominous pulses,
All day, the commotion of sinewy, mane-tossing
    horses;
All night, from their cells, the importunate tramping
    and neighing.*

We spur to a land of no name, out-racing the storm-
　　wind;
We leap to the infinite dark, like the sparks from the
　　anvil.
Thou leadest, O God! All's well with thy troopers
　　that follow.

ARTHUR GUITERMAN
1871—

HILLS

I NEVER loved your plains!—
　　Your gentle valleys,
Your drowsy country lanes
　　And pleachèd alleys.

I want my hills!—the trail
　　That scorns the hollow.—
Up, up the ragged shale
　　Where few will follow,

Up, over wooded crest
　　And mossy boulder
With strong thigh, heaving chest,
　　And swinging shoulder,

So let me hold my way,
　　By nothing halted,
Until, at close of day,
　　I stand, exalted,

High on my hills of dream—
　　Dear hills that know me!
And then, how fair will seem
　　The lands below me,

ARTHUR GUITERMAN

How pure, at vesper-time,
    The far bells chiming—
God, give me hills to climb
    And strength for climbing!

STRICTLY GERM-PROOF

THE Antiseptic Baby and the Prophylactic Pup
Were playing in the garden when the Bunny gam-
    boled up;
They looked upon the Creature with a loathing undis-
    guised;—
It wasn't Disinfected and it wasn't Sterilized.

They said it was a Microbe and a Hotbed of Disease;
They steamed it in a vapor of a thousand-odd de-
    grees;
They froze it in a freezer that was cold as Banished
    Hope
And washed it in permanganate with carbolated soap.

In sulphureted hydrogen they steeped its wiggly ears;
They trimmed its frisky whiskers with a pair of
    hard-boiled shears;
They donned their rubber mittens and they took it
    by the hand
And 'lected it a member of the Fumigated Band.

There's not a Micrococcus in the garden where they
    play;
They bathe in pure iodoform a dozen times a day;
And each imbibes his rations from a Hygienic Cup—
The Bunny and the Baby and the Prophylactic Pup.

FITZ GREENE HALLECK
1790—1867

MARCO BOZZARIS

At midnight, in his guarded tent,
  The Turk was dreaming of the hour
When Greece, her knee in suppliance bent,
  Should tremble at his power:
In dreams, through camp and court, he bore
The trophies of a conqueror;
  In dreams his song of triumph heard;
Then wore his monarch's signet ring:
Then pressed that monarch's throne—a king;
As wild his thoughts, and gay of wing,
  As Eden's garden bird.

At midnight, in the forest shades,
  Bozzaris ranged his Suliote band,
True as the steel of their tried blades,
  Heroes in heart and hand.
There had the Persian's thousands stood,
There had the glad earth drunk their blood
  On old Platæa's day;
And now there breathed that haunted air
The sons of sires who conquered there,
With arm to strike and soul to dare,
  As quick, as far as they.

An hour passed on—the Turk awoke;
  That bright dream was his last;
He woke—to hear his sentries shriek,
"To arms! they come! the Greek! the Greek!"

He woke—to die midst flame, and smoke,
And shout, and groan, and sabre-stroke,
   And death-shots falling thick and fast
As lightnings from the mountain-cloud;
And heard, with voice as trumpet loud,
   Bozzaris cheer his band:
"Strike—till the last armed foe expires;
Strike—for your altars and your fires;
Strike—for the green graves of your sires;
   God—and your native land!"

They fought—like brave men, long and well;
   They piled that ground with Moslem slain,
They conquered—but Bozzaris fell,
   Bleeding at every vein.
His few surviving comrades saw
His smile when rang their proud hurrah,
   And the red field was won;
Then saw in death his eyelids close
Calmly, as to a night's repose,
   Like flowers at set of sun.

Come to the bridal-chamber, Death!
   Come to the mother's, when she feels,
For the first time, her first-born's breath;
   Come when the blessed seals
That close the pestilence are broke,
And crowded cities wail its stroke;
Come in consumption's ghastly form,
The earthquake shock, the ocean storm;
Come when the heart beats high and warm
   With banquet-song, and dance, and wine;
And thou art terrible—the tear,

The groan, the knell, the pall, the bier,
And all we know, or dream, or fear
   Of agony, are thine.

But to the hero, when his sword
   Has won the battle for the free,
Thy voice sounds like a prophet's word;
   And in its hollow tones are heard
     The thanks of millions yet to be.
Come, when his task of fame is wrought—
Come, with her laurel-leaf, blood-bought—
   Come in her crowning hour—and then
Thy sunken eye's unearthly light
To him is welcome as the sight
   Of sky and stars to prisoned men;
Thy grasp is welcome as the hand
Of brother in a foreign land;
Thy summons welcome as the cry
That told the Indian isles were nigh
   To the world-seeking Genoese,
When the land wind, from woods of palm,
And orange-groves, and fields of balm,
   Blew o'er the Haytian seas.

Bozzaris! with the storied brave
   Greece nurtured in her glory's time,
Rest thee—there is no prouder grave,
   Even in her own proud clime,
She wore no funeral-weeds for thee,
   Nor bade the dark hearse wave its plume
Like torn branch from death's leafless tree
In sorrow's pomp and pageantry,
   The heartless luxury of the tomb;

But she remembers thee as one
Long loved and for a season gone;
For thee her poet's lyre is wreathed,
Her marble wrought, her music breathed;
For thee she rings the birthday bells;
Of thee her babe's first lisping tells;
For thine her evening prayer is said
At palace-couch and cottage-bed;
Her soldier, closing with the foe,
Gives for thy sake a deadlier blow;
His plighted maiden, when she fears
For him the joy of her young years,
Thinks of thy fate, and checks her tears;
   And she, the mother of thy boys,
Though in her eye and faded cheek
Is read the grief she will not speak,
   The memory of her buried joys,
And even she who gave thee birth,
Will, by their pilgrim-circled hearth,
   Talk of thy doom without a sigh;
For thou art Freedom's now, and Fame's:
One of the few, the immortal names,
   That were not born to die.

ON THE DEATH OF JOSEPH RODMAN DRAKE

GREEN be the turf above thee,
   Friend of my better days!
None knew thee but to love thee,
   Nor named thee but to praise.

Tears fell when thou wert dying,
   From eyes unused to weep,

And long, where thou art lying,
   Will tears the cold turf steep.

When hearts, whose truth was proven,
   Like thine, are laid in earth,
There should a wreath be woven
   To tell the world their worth;

And I who woke each morrow
   To clasp thy hand in mine,
Who shared thy joy and sorrow,
   Whose weal and woe were thine;

It should be mine to braid it
   Around thy faded brow,
But I've in vain essayed it,
   And feel I cannot now.

While memory bids me weep thee,
   Nor thoughts nor words are free,—
The grief is fixed too deeply
   That mourns a man like thee.

JOEL CHANDLER HARRIS
1848—1903

MY HONEY, MY LOVE

Hit's a mighty fur ways up de Far'well Lane,
   My honey, my love!
You may ax Mister Crow, you may ax Mister Crane,
   My honey, my love!
Dey'll make you a bow, en dey'll tell you de same,
   My honey, my love!

Hit's a mighty fur ways fer ter go in de night,
  My honey, my love!
My honey, my love, my heart's delight—
  My honey, my love!

Mister Mink, he creeps twel he wake up de snipe,
  My honey, my love!
Mister Bull-Frog holler, Come alight my pipe!
  My honey, my love!
En de Pa'tridge ax, Ain't yo' peas ripe?
  My honey, my love!
Better not walk erlong dar much atter night,
  My honey, my love!
My honey, my love, my heart's delight—
  My honey, my love!

De Bully-Bat fly mighty close ter de groun',
  My honey, my love!
Mister Fox, he coax 'er, Do come down!
  My honey, my love!
Mister Coon, he rack all 'roun' 'en 'roun',
  My honey, my love!
In de darkes' night, oh, de nigger, he's a sight!
  My honey, my love!
My honey, my love, my heart's delight—
  My honey, my love!

Oh, flee, Miss Nancy, flee ter my knee,
  My honey, my love!
'Lev'n big, fat coons liv' in one tree,
  My honey, my love!
Oh, ladies all, won't you marry me?
  My honey, my love!

Tu'n lef', t'un right, we'll dance all night,
My honey, my love!
My honey, my love, my heart's delight—
My honey, my love!

De big Owl holler en cry fer his mate,
My honey, my love!
Oh, don't stay long! Oh, don't stay late!
My honey, my love!
Hit ain't so mighty fur ter de Good-by Gate,
My honey, my love!
Whar we all got ter go w'en we sing out de night,
My honey, my love!
My honey, my love, my heart's delight—
My honey, my love!

BRET HARTE

1839—1902

SAN FRANCISCO

(FROM THE SEA)

SERENE, indifferent of Fate,
Thou sittest at the Western Gate;

Upon thy height, so lately won,
Still slant the banners of the sun;

Thou seest the white seas strike their tents,
O Warder of two continents!

And, scornful of the peace that flies
Thy angry winds and sullen skies,

Thou drawest all things, small or great,
To thee, beside the Western Gate.

      .   .

O lion's whelp, that hidest fast
In jungle growth of spire and mast!

I know thy cunning and thy greed,
Thy hard high lust and willful deed,

And all thy glory loves to tell
Of specious gifts material.

Drop down, O Fleecy Fog, and hide
Her skeptic sneer and all her pride!

Wrap her, O Fog, in gown and hood
Of her Franciscan Brotherhood.

Hide me her faults, her sin and blame;
With thy gray mantle cloak her shame!

So shall she, cowlèd, sit and pray
Till morning bears her sins away.

Then rise, O Fleecy Fog, and raise
The glory of her coming days;

Be as the cloud that flecks the seas
Above her smoky argosies;

When forms familiar shall give place
To stranger speech and newer face;

When all her throes and anxious fears
Lie hushed in the repose of years;

When Art shall raise and Culture lift
The sensual joys and meaner thrift,

And all fulfilled the vision we
Who watch and wait shall never see;

Who, in the morning of her race,
Toiled fair or meanly in our place,

But, yielding to the common lot,
Lie unrecorded and forgot.

THE HEATHEN CHINEE

WHICH I wish to remark,
  And my language is plain,
That for ways that are dark
  And for tricks that are vain,
The heathen Chinee is peculiar,
  Which the same I would rise to explain.

Ah Sin was his name;
  And I shall not deny,
In regard to the same,
  What that name might imply;
But his smile it was pensive and childlike,
  As I frequent remarked to Bill Nye.

It was August the third,
  And quite soft was the skies;
Which it might be inferred
  That Ah Sin was likewise;

Yet he played it that day upon William
   And me in a way I despise.

Which we had a small game,
   And Ah Sin took a hand:
It was Euchre. The same
   He did not understand;
But he smiled as he sat by the table,
   With the smile that was childlike and bland.

Yet the cards they were stocked
   In a way that I grieve,
And my feelings were shocked,
   At the state of Nye's sleeve,
Which was stuffed full of aces and bowers,
   And the same with intent to deceive.

But the hands that were played
   By that heathen Chinee,
And the points that he made,
   Were quite frightful to see,—
Till at last he put down a right bower,
   Which the same Nye had dealt unto me.

Then I looked up at Nye,
   And he gazed upon me;
And he rose with a sigh,
   And said, "Can this be?
We are ruined by Chinese cheap labor,"—
   And he went for that heathen Chinee.

In the scene that ensued
   I did not take a hand,

But the floor it was strewed
  Like the leaves on the strand
With the cards that Ah Sin had been hiding,
  In the game "he did not understand."

In his sleeves, which were long,
  He had twenty-four packs,—
Which was coming it strong,
  Yet I state but the facts;
And we found on his nails, which were taper,
  What is frequent in tapers,—that's wax.

Which is why I remark,
  And my language is plain,
That for ways that are dark
  And for tricks that are vain,
The heathen Chinee is peculiar,—
  Which the same I am free to maintain.

THE AGED STRANGER

"I was with Grant"—the stranger said;
  Said the farmer, "Say no more,
But rest thee here at my cottage porch,
  For thy feet are weary and sore."

"I was with Grant"—the stranger said;
  Said the farmer, "Nay, no more,—
I prithee sit at my frugal board,
  And eat of my humble store.

"How fares my boy,—my soldier boy,
  Of the old Ninth Army Corps?
I warrant he bore him gallantly
  In the smoke and the battle's roar!"

"I know him not," said the aged man,
  "And, as I remarked before,
I was with Grant"— "Nay, nay, I know,"
  Said the farmer, "say no more:

"He fell in battle,—I see, alas!
  Thou 'dst smooth these tidings o'er,—
Nay, speak the truth, whatever it be,
  Though it rend my bosom's core.

"How fell he? With his face to the foe,
  Upholding the flag he bore?
Oh, say not that my boy disgraced
  The uniform that he wore!"

"I cannot tell," said the aged man,
  "And should have remarked before,
That I was with Grant,—in Illinois,—
  Some three years before the war."

Then the farmer spake him never a word,
  But beat with his fist full sore
That aged man who had worked for Grant
  Some three years before the war.

HER LETTER

I'M sitting alone by the fire,
  Dressed just as I came from the dance,
In a robe even *you* would admire,—
  It cost a cool thousand in France;
I'm be-diamonded out of all reason,
  My hair is done up in a cue:
In short, sir. "the belle of the season"
  Is wasting an hour upon you.

A dozen engagements I've broken;
  I left in the midst of a set;
Likewise a proposal, half spoken,
  That waits—on the stairs—for me yet.
They say he'll be rich,—when he grows up,
  And then he adores me indeed;
And you, sir, are turning your nose up,
  Three thousand miles off, as you read.

"And how do I like my position?"
  "And what do I think of New York?"
"And now, in my higher ambition,
    With whom do I waltz, flirt, or talk?"
"And isn't it nice to have riches,
  And diamonds and silks, and all that?"
"And aren't they a change to the ditches
  And tunnels of Poverty Flat?"

Well, yes,—if you saw us out driving
  Each day in the Park, four-in-hand,
If you saw poor dear mamma contriving
  To look supernaturally grand,—
If you saw papa's picture, as taken
  By Brady, and tinted at that,—
You'd never suspect he sold bacon
  And flour at Poverty Flat.

And yet, just this moment, when sitting
  In the glare of the grand chandelier,—
In the bustle and glitter befitting
  The "finest *soirée* of the year,"—

In the mists of a *gaze de Chambéry,*
  And the hum of the smallest of talk,—
Somehow, Joe, I thought of the "Ferry,"
  And the dance that we had on "The Fork";

Of Harrison's barn, with its muster
  Of flags festooned over the wall;
Of the candles that shed their soft lustre
  And tallow on head-dress and shawl;
Of the steps that we took to one fiddle,
  Of the dress of my queer *vis-à-vis;*
And how I once went down the middle
  With the man that shot Sandy McGee;

Of the moon that was quietly sleeping
  On the hill, when the time came to go;
Of the few baby peaks that were peeping
  From under their bedclothes of snow;
Of that ride—that to me was the rarest;
  Of—the something you said at the gate
Ah! Joe, then I wasn't an heiress
  To "the best-paying lead in the State."

Well, well, it's all past; yet it's funny
  To think, as I stood in the glare
Of fashion and beauty and money,
  That I should be thinking, right there,
Of some one who breasted high water,
  And swam the North Fork, and all that,
Just to dance with old Folinsbee's daughter,
  The Lily of Poverty Flat.

But goodness! what nonsense I'm writing!
  (Mamma says my taste still is low),

Instead of my triumphs reciting,
 I'm spooning on Joseph,—heigh-ho!
And I'm to be "finished" by travel,—
 Whatever's the meaning of that.
Oh, why did papa strike pay gravel
 In drifting on Poverty Flat?

Good-night!—here's the end of my paper;
 Good-night!—if the longitude please,—
For maybe, while wasting my taper,
 Your sun's climbing over the trees.
But know, if you haven't got riches,
 And are poor, dearest Joe, and all that,
That my heart's somewhere there in the ditches,
 And you've struck it,—on Poverty Flat.

ROBERT STEPHEN HAWKER
1804—1875

THE SONG OF THE WESTERN MEN

A GOOD sword and a trusty hand!
 A merry heart and true!
King James's men shall understand
 What Cornish lads can do.

And have they fix'd the where and when?
 And shall Trelawny die?
Here's twenty thousand Cornish men
 Will know the reason why!

Out spake their captain brave and bold,
 A merry wight was he:
"If London Tower were Michael's hold,
 We'll set Trelawny free!

JOHN HAY

"We'll cross the Tamar, land to land,
  The Severn is no stay,
With 'one and all,' and hand in hand,
  And who shall bid us nay?

"And when we come to London Wall,
  A pleasant sight to view,
Come forth! come forth, ye cowards all,
  Here's men as good as you!

"Trelawny he's in keep and hold,
  Trelawny he may die;
But here's twenty thousand Cornish bold,
  Will know the reason why!"

JOHN HAY
1838—1905

JIM BLUDSO

WAL, no! I can't tell whar he lives,
  Because he don't live, you see;
Leastways, he's got out of the habit
  Of livin' like you and me.
Whar have you been for the last three years
  That you haven't heard folks tell
How Jemmy Bludso passed-in his checks,
  The night of the Prairie Belle?

He weren't no saint—them engineers
  Is all pretty much alike—
One wife in Natchez-under-the-Hill,
  And another one here in Pike.

A keerless man in his talk was Jim,
    And an awkward man in a row—
But he never flunked, and he never lied;
    I reckon he never knowed how.

And this was all the religion he had—
    To treat his engines well;
Never be passed on the river;
    To mind the pilot's bell;
And if ever the Prairie Belle took fire,
    A thousand times he swore,
He'd hold her nozzle agin the bank
    Till the last soul got ashore.

All boats have their day on the Mississip,
    And her day come at last.
The Movastar was a better boat,
    But the Belle she wouldn't be passed;
And so come tearin' along that night,—
    The oldest craft on the line,
With a nigger squat on her safety valve,
    And her furnace crammed, rosin and pine.

The fire bust out as she clared the bar,
    And burnt a hole in the night,
And quick as a flash she turned, and made
    To that willer-bank on the right.
There was runnin' and cursin', but Jim yelled out
    Over all the infernal roar,
"I'll hold her nozzle agin the bank
    Till the last galoot's ashore."

Through the hot black breath of the burnin' boat
    Jim Bludso's voice was heard,

And they all had trust in his cussedness,
  And know he would keep his word.
And, sure's you're born, they all got off
  Afore the smokestacks fell,—
And Bludso's ghost went up alone
  In the smoke of the Prairie Belle.

He weren't no saint—but at jedgment
  I'd run my chance with Jim,
'Longside of some pious gentlemen
  That wouldn't shook hands with him.
He'd seen his duty, a dead-sure thing—
  And went for it thar and then:
And Christ ain't a going to be too hard
  On a man that died for men.

LITTLE BREECHES

I DON'T go much on religion,
  I never ain't had no show;
But I've got a middlin' tight grip, sir,
  On a handful o' things I know.
I don't pan out on the prophets
  And free-will and that sort of thing—
But I be'lieve in God and the angels,
  Ever sence one night last spring.

I come into town with some turnips,
  And my little Gabe come along—
No four-year-old in the county
  Could beat him for pretty and strong—
Peart and chipper and sassy,
  Always ready to swear and fight—

And I'd larnt him to chaw terbacker
    Jest to keep his milk-teeth white.

The snow come down like a blanket
    As I passed by Taggart's store;
I went in for a jug of molasses
    And left the team at the door.
They scared at something and started—
    I heard one little squall,
And hell-to-split over the prairie!
    Went team, Little Breeches, and all,

Hell-to-split over the prairie!
    I was almost froze with skeer;
But we rousted up some torches,
    And sarched for 'em far and near.
At last we struck hosses and wagon,
    Snowed under a soft white mound,
Upsot, dead beat, but of little Gabe
    No hide nor hair was found.

And here all hope soured on me
    Of my fellow-critter's aid;
I jest flopped down on my marrow-bones,
    Crotch-deep in the snow, and prayed.

By this, the torches was played out,
    And me and Isrul Parr
Went off from some wood to a sheepfold
    That he said was somewhar thar.

We found it at last, and a little shed
    Where they shut up the lambs at night;

We looked in and seen them huddled thar,
  So warm and sleepy and white;
And thar sot Little Breeches and chirped,
  As peart as ever you see,
"I want a chaw of terbacker,
  And that's what's the matter of me."

How did he git thar? Angels.
  He could never have walked in that storm:
They jest scooped down and toted him
  To what it was safe and warm.
And I think that saving a little child,
  And fotching him to his own,
Is a derned sight better business
  Than loafing around the Throne.

REGINALD HEBER
1783—1826
HOLY, HOLY, HOLY!

HOLY, holy, holy, LORD GOD Almighty!
  Early in the morning our song shall rise to Thee;
Holy, holy, holy! merciful and mighty!
  GOD in Three Persons, blessèd TRINITY!

Holy, holy, holy! all the saints adore Thee,
  Casting down their golden crowns around the
    glassy sea;
Cherubin and Seraphim falling down before Thee,
  Which wert and art and evermore shalt be!

Holy, holy, holy! Though the darkness hide Thee,
  Though the eye of sinful man Thy glory may not
    see,

Only Thou art holy, there is none beside Thee,
    Perfect in power, in love, and purity!

Holy, holy, holy, LORD GOD Almighty!
    All Thy works shall praise Thy Name in earth
        and sky and sea:—
Holy, holy, holy! Merciful and mighty!
    GOD in Three Persons, blesséd TRINITY!

HEINRICH HEINE
1797—1856

GERMANY

LORELEY

I WIST not what it is daunts me,
    And makes me feel eerie and low:
A legend, it troubles, it haunts me,
    A legend of long ago.

The air chills, day is declining,
    And smoothly Rhine's waters run,
And the peaks of the mountains are shining
    Aloft in the setting sun.

A maiden of wondrous seeming,
    Most beautiful, see, sits there;
Her jewels in gold are gleaming,
    She combs out her golden hair.

With a comb of red gold she parts it,
    And still as she combs it she sings;
As the melody falls on our hearts, it
    With power as of magic stings.

With a spasm the boatman hears it
  Out there in his little skiff:
He sees not the reef as he nears it,
  He only looks up to the cliff.

The waters will sweep, I am thinking,
  O'er skiff, ay, and boatman ere long;
And this is, when daylight is sinking,
  What Loreley did with her song.

Translated by T. Martin

THE GRENADIERS

FOR France two grenadiers held their way,
  Had prisoners been in Russia;
And sorrowful men they were, when they
  The frontier reached of Prussia.

For there they heard of a dire event,—
  How the world 'gainst France had risen, her
Grande armée had shattered and shent,
  And taken her Emperor prisoner.

They mingled their tears, these two grenadiers,
  To the sad tale ever returning:
"Oh would!" said one, "that my days were done!
  My old wounds, how they're burning!"

"All's up!" said the other; "and sooner than not
  I would die like you, never doubt me;
But a wife and child at home I've got,
  And they must be starved without me!"

"Hang wife and child! It is something more,
  And better far, that I pant for;
My Emperor prisoner! My Emperor!
  Let them go beg what they want for!

"If I die just now, as 'tis like I may,
  Then, comrade, this boon grant me,
Take my body with you to France away,
  And in France's dear earth plant me.

"The *Croix d'Honneur*, with its crimson band,
  On my heart see that you place it;
Then give me my rifle in my hand,
  And my sword, around me brace it.

"So will I lie, and listen all ear,
  Like a sentinel, low in my bed there,
Till the roar of the cannon some day I hear,
  And the neigh of the steeds as they tread there.

"Then I'll know 'tis my Emperor riding by;
  Many sabres are flashing toward him,
And out from my grace full armed spring I,
  The Emperor! to shield and to guard him!"

Translated by T. Martin.

"DU BIST WIE EINE BLUME"

THOU art even as a flower is,
  So gentle, and pure, and fair;
I gaze on thee, and sadness
  Comes over my heart unaware.

≫ 38 ≪

I feel as though I should lay, sweet,
  My hands on thy head, with a prayer
That God may keep thee alway, sweet,
  As gentle, and pure, and fair!

Translated by T. Martin.

BELSHAZZAR

THE midnight hour was drawing on;
Hushed into rest lay Babylon.

All save the royal palace, where
Was the din of revel, and torches' flare.

There high within his royal hall
Belshazzar the king held festival.

His nobles around him in splendour shine,
And drain down goblets of sparkling wine.

The nobles shout, and the goblets ring;
'Twas sweet to the heart of that stiff-neck'd king.

The cheeks of the king, they flushed with flame,
As he drank, he grew bolder, more dead to shame.

And, madden'd with pride, his lips let fall
Wild words, that blaspheme the great Lord of All.

More vaunting he grew, and his blasphemous sneers
Were hailed by his lordly rout with cheers.

Proudly the king has a mandate passed;
Away hie the slaves, and come back full fast.

Many gold vessels they bring with them,
The spoils of God's House in Jerusalem.

With impious hand the king caught up,
Filled to the brim, a sacred cup;

And down to the bottom he drain'd it dry,
And with mouth a-foam thus aloud did cry,—

"Jehovah! I scoff at Thy greatness gone.
I am the king of Babylon!"

The terrible words were ringing still,
When the king at his heart felt a secret chill.

The laughter ceased, the lords held their breath
And all through the hall it was still as death.

And see, see there! on the white wall, see,
Comes forth what seems a man's hand to be!

And it wrote and wrote in letters of flame
On the white wall,—then vanished the way it came.

The king sat staring, he could not speak,
His knees knocked together, death-pale was his
    cheek.

With cold fear creeping his lords sat round,
They sat dumb-stricken, with never a sound.

The Magians came, yet not one of them all
Could read the flame-writing upon the wall.

But or ever that night did to morning wane,
Belshazzar the king by his lords was slain.

Translated by T. Martin.

FELICIA HEMANS
1793—1835

THE HOMES OF ENGLAND

> "Where's the coward that would not dare
> To fight for such a land?—*Marmion.*

THE stately homes of England,
  How beautiful they stand,
Amidst their tall ancestral trees,
  O'er all the pleasant land!
The deer across their greensward bound,
  Through shade and sunny gleam;
And the swan glides past them with the sound
  Of some rejoicing stream.

The merry homes of England!
  Around their hearths by night,
What gladsome looks of household love
  Meet in the ruddy light!
There woman's voice flows forth in song,
  Or childhood's tale is told,
Or lips move tunefully along
  Some glorious page of old.

The blessed homes of England!
  How softly on their bowers
Is laid the holy quietness
  That breathes from Sabbath hours!
Solemn, yet sweet, the church-bell's chime
  Floats through their woods at morn;
All other sounds, in that still time,
  Of breeze and leaf are born.

The cottage homes of England!
  By thousands on her plains,
They are smiling o'er the silvery brooks,
  And round the hamlet fanes.
Through glowing orchards forth they peep,
  Each from its nook of leaves;
And fearless there the lowly sleep,
  As the bird beneath their eaves.

The free fair homes of England!
  Long, long, in hut and hall,
May hearts of native proof be reared
  To guard each hallowed wall!
And green for ever be the groves,
  And bright the flowery sod,
Where first the child's glad spirit loves
  Its country and its God!

THE LANDING OF THE PILGRIM FATHERS

THE breaking waves dashed high
  On a stern and rock-bound coast,
And the woods, against a stormy sky,
  Their giant branches tost:

And the heavy night hung dark
  The hills and water o'er,
When a band of exiles moored their bark
  On the wild New England shore.

Not as the conqueror comes,
  They, the true-hearted, came,
Not with the roll of the stirring drums,
  And the trumpet that sings of fame;

Not as the flying come,
  In silence and in fear,—
They shook the depths of the desert's gloom,
  With their hymns of lofty cheer.

Amidst the storm they sang,
  And the stars heard and the sea!
And the sounding aisles of the dim woods rang
  To the anthem of the free.

The ocean-eagle soared
  From his nest by the white wave's foam,
And the rocking pines of the forest roared—
  This was their welcome home!

There were men with hoary hair,
  Amidst that pilgrim-band—
Why had they come to wither there
  Away from their childhood's land?

There was woman's fearless eye,
  Lit by her deep love's truth;
There was manhood's brow serenely high,
  And the fiery heart of youth.

What sought they thus afar?
  Bright jewels of the mine?
The wealth of seas, the spoils of war?—
  They sought a faith's pure shrine!

Ay, call it holy ground,
  The soil where first they trod!
They have left unstained what there they found—
  Freedom to worship God!

CASABIANCA

THE boy stood on the burning deck
  Whence all but he had fled;
The flame that lit the battle's wreck
  Shone round him o'er the dead.

Yet beautiful and bright he stood,
  As born to rule the storm—
A creature of heroic blood,
  A proud, though childlike form.

The flames rolled on—he would not go
  Without his father's word;
That father, faint in death below,
  His voice no longer heard.

He called aloud:—"Say, father, say
  If yet my task is done!"
He knew not that the chieftain lay
  Unconscious of his son.

"Speak, father!" once again he cried,
  If I may yet be gone!"
And but the booming shots replied,
And fast the flames rolled on.

Upon his brow he felt their breath,
  And in his waving hair,
And looked from that lone post of death
  In still yet brave despair;

And shouted but once more aloud,
  "My father! must I stay?"
While o'er him fast, through sail and shroud,
  The wreathing fires made way.

They wrapt the ship in splendour wild,
  They caught the flag on high,
And streamed above the gallant child
  Like banners in the sky.

There came a burst of thunder-sound—
  The boy—oh! where was he?
Ask of the winds that far around
  With fragments strewed the sea!—

With mast, and helm, and pennon fair,
  That well had borne their part;
But the noblest thing which perished there
  Was that young faithful heart!

WILLIAM E. HENLEY

1849—1903

THE CHRISTIAN SLAVE

Or ever the knightly years were gone
  With the old world to the grave,
I was a King in Babylon
  And you were a Christian Slave.

I saw, I took, I cast you by,
  I bent and broke your pride.
You loved me well, or I heard them lie,
  But your longing was denied.
Surely I knew that by and by
  You cursed your gods and died.

And a myriad suns have set and shone
    Since then upon the grave
Decreed by the King in Babylon
    To her that had been his Slave.

The pride I trampled is now my scathe,
    For it tramples me again.
The old resentment lasts like death,
    For you love, yet you refrain.
I break my heart on your hard unfaith,
    And I break my heart in vain.

Yet not for an hour do I wish undone
    The deed beyond the grave,
When I was a King in Babylon
    And you were a Virgin Slave.

SONG OF THE SWORD

The Sword
Singing—
The voice of the Sword from the heart of the Sword
Clanging imperious
Forth from Time's battlements
His ancient and triumphing Song.

In the beginning,
Ere God inspired Himself
Into the clay thing
Thumbed to His image,
The vacant, the naked shell
Soon to be Man:

WILLIAM E. HENLEY

Thoughtful He pondered it,
Prone there and impotent,
Fragile, inviting
Attack and discomfiture;
Then, with a smile—
As He heard in the Thunder
That laughed over Eden
The voice of the Trumpet,
The iron Beneficence,
Calling his dooms
To the Winds of the world—
Stooping, He drew
On the sand with His finger
A shape for a sign
Of his way to the eyes
That in wonder should waken,
For a proof of His will
To the breaking intelligence.
That was the birth of me:
I am the Sword.

Bleak and lean, gray and cruel,
Short-hilted, long-shafted,
I froze into steel;
And the blood of my elder,
His hand on the hafts of me,
Sprang like a wave
In the wind, as the sense
Of his strength grew to ecstasy;
Glowed like a coal
In the throat of the furnace;
As he knew me and named me
The War-Thing, the Comrade,

Father of honour
And giver of kingship,
The fame-smith, the song-master,
Bringer of women
On fire at his hands
For the pride of fulfilment,
Priest (saith the Lord)
Of his marriage with victory.
Ho! then, the Trumpet,
Handmaid of heroes,
Calling the peers
To the place of espousals!
Ho! then, the splendour
And glare of my ministry,
Clothing the earth
With a livery of lightnings!
Ho! then, the music
Of battles in onset,
And ruining armours,
And God's gift returning
In fury to God!
Thrilling and keen
As the song of the winter stars,
Ho, then, the sound
Of my voice, the implacable
Angel of Destiny!—
I am the Sword.

Heroes, my children,
Follow, O, follow me!
Follow, exulting
In the great light that breaks
From the sacred Companionship!

Thrust through the fatuous,
Thrust through the fungous **brood**,
Spawned in my shadow
And gross with my gift!
Thrust through, and hearken,
O, hark, to the Trumpet,
The Virgin of Battles,
Calling, still calling you
Into the Presence,
Sons of the Judgment,
Pure wafts of the Will!
Edged to annihilate,
Hilted with government,
Follow, O, follow me,
Till the waste places
All the gray globe over
Ooze, as the honeycomb
Drips, with the sweetness
Distilled of my strength,
And, teeming in peace
Through the wrath of my coming,
They give back in beauty
The dread and the anguish
They had of me visitant!
Follow, O follow, then,
Heroes, my harvesters!
Where the tall grain is ripe
Thrust in your sickles!
Stripped and adust
In a stubble of empire,
Scything and binding
The full sheaves of sovranty:
Thus, O, thus gloriously,

Shall you fulfil yourselves!
Thus, O, thus mightily,
Show yourselves sons of mine—
Yea, and win grace of me:
I am the Sword!

I am the feast-maker:
Hark, through a noise
Of the screaming of eagles,
Hark how the Trumpet,
The mistress of mistresses,
Calls, silver-throated
And stern, where the tables
Are spread, and the meal
Of the Lord is in hand!
Driving the darkness,
Even as the banners
And spears of the Morning;
Sifting the nations,
The slag from the metal,
The waste and the weak
From the fit and the strong;
Fighting the brute,
The abysmal Fecundity;
Checking the gross,
Multitudinous blunders,
The groping, the purblind
Excesses in service
Of the Womb universal,
The absolute drudge;
Firing the charactry
Carved on the World,
The miraculous gem

In the seal-ring that burns
On the hand of the Master—
Yea! and authority
Flames through the dim,
Unappeasable Grisliness
Prone down the nethermost
Chasms of the Void!—
Clear singing, clean slicing;
Sweet spoken, soft finishing;
Making death beautiful,
Life but a coin
To be staked in the pastime
Whose playing is more
Than the transfer of being;
Arch-anarch, chief builder,
Prince and evangelist,
I am the Will of God:
I am the Sword.
The Sword
Singing—
The voice of the Sword from the heart of the
Sword
Clanging majestical,
As from the starry-staired
Courts of the primal Supremacy,
His high, irresistible song.

INVICTUS

Out of the night that covers me,
    Black as the pit from pole to pole,
I thank whatever gods may be
    For my unconquerable soul.

In the fell clutch of circumstance
  I have not winced nor cried aloud.
Under the bludgeonings of chance
  My head is bloody, but unbowed.

Beyond this place of wrath and tears
  Looms but the Horror of the shade,
And yet the menace of the years
  Finds and shall find me unafraid.

It matters not how strait the gate,
  How charged with punishments the scroll,
I am the master of my fate:
  I am the captain of my soul.

MIDSUMMER DAYS AND NIGHTS

To W. H.

WITH a ripple of leaves and a tinkle of streams
The full world rolls in a rhythm of praise,
And the winds are one with the clouds and beams—
Midsummer days! Midsummer days!
The dusk grows vast; in a purple haze,
While the West from a rapture of sunset rights,
Faint stars their exquisite lamps upraise—
Midsummer nights! O midsummer nights!

The wood's green heart is a nest of dreams,
The lush grass thickens and springs and sways,
The rathe wheat rustles, the landscape gleams—
Midsummer days! Midsummer days!

In the stilly fields, in the stilly ways,
All secret shadows and mystic lights,
Late lovers murmur and linger and gaze—
Midsummer nights! O midsummer nights!

There's a music of bells from the trampling teams,
Wild skylarks hover, the gorses blaze,
The rich, ripe rose as with incense steams—
Midsummer days! Midsummer days!
A soul from the honeysuckle strays,
And the nightingale as from prophet heights
Sings to the Earth of her million Mays—
Midsummer nights! O midsummer nights!

ENVOY

And it's O, for my dear and the charm that stays—
Midsummer days! Midsummer days!
It's O, for my Love and the dark that plights—
Midsummer nights! O midsummer nights!

GEORGE HERBERT
1593—1632
DISCIPLINE

THROW away Thy rod,
Throw away Thy wrath;
   O my GOD,
Take the gentle path.

For my heart's desire
Unto Thine is bent;
   I aspire
To a full consent.

Though I fail, I weep;
Though I halt in pace,
  Yet I creep
To the throne of grace.

Then let wrath remove;
Love will do the deed;
  For with love
Stony hearts will bleed.

Love is swift of foot;
Love's a man of war,
  And can shoot,
And can hit from far.

Who can 'scape his bow?
That which wrought on Thee,
  Brought Thee low,
Needs must work on me.

Throw away Thy rod:
Though man frailties hath,
  Thou art GOD;
Throw away Thy wrath.

ROBERT HERRICK
1591—1674

TO THE VIRGINS, TO MAKE MUCH OF TIME

GATHER ye Rose-buds while ye may,
 Old Time is still a flying:
And this same flower that smiles to day,
 To morrow will be dying.

The glorious Lamp of Heaven, the Sun,
   The higher he's a getting;
The sooner will his Race be run,
   And neerer he's to Setting.

That Age is best, which is the first,
   When Youth and Blood are warmer;
But being spent, the worse, and worst
   Times, still succeed the former.

Then be not coy, but use your time;
   And while ye may, goe marry:
For having lost but once your prime,
   You may for ever tarry.

TO DAFFADILLS

FAIRE Daffadills, we weep to see
   You haste away so soone:
As yet the early-rising Sun
   Has not attain'd his Noone.
     Stay, stay,
   Untill the hasting day
     Has run
   But to the Even-song;
And, having pray'd together, we
    Will goe with you along.

We have short time to stay, as you,
   We have as short a Spring;
As quick a growth to meet Decay,
   As you, or any thing.
     We die,

As yours doe, and drie
         Away,
Like to the Summers raine;
Or as the pearles of Mornings dew
         Ne'r to be found againe.

THE NIGHT-PIECE, TO JULIA

HER Eyes the Glow-worme lend thee,
The Shooting Starres attend thee
         And the Elves also,
         Whose little eyes glow,
Like the sparks of fire, befriend thee.

No *Will-o'-th'-Wispe* mis-light thee;
Nor Snake, or Slow-worme bite thee:
         But on, on thy way
         Not making a stay,
Since Ghost ther's none to affright thee.

Let not the darke thee cumber;
What though the Moon do's slumber?
         The Starres of the night,
         Will lend thee their light,
Like Tapers cleare without number.

Then *Julia* let me wooe thee,
Thus, thus to come unto me:
         And when I shall meet
         Thy silv'ry feet,
My soule Ile poure into thee.

ROBERT HERRICK

A TERNARIE OF LITTLES, UPON A PIPKIN OF JELLIE SENT TO A LADY

A LITTLE Saint best fits a little Shrine,
A little prop best fits a little Vine,
As my small Cruse best fits my little Wine.

A little Seed best fits a little Soyle,
A little Trade best fits a little Toyle:
As my small Jarre best fits my little Oyle.

A little Bin best fits a little Bread,
A little Garland fits a little Head:
As my small stuffe best fits my little Shed.

A little Hearth best fits a little Fire,
A little Chappell fits a little Quire,
As my small Bell best fits my little Spire.

A little streame best fits a little Boat;
A little lead best fits a little Float;
As my small Pipe best fits my little note.

A little meat best fits a little bellie,
As sweetly Lady, give me leave to tell ye
This little Pipkin fits this little Jellie.

CHERRIE-RIPE

CHERRIE-RIPE, Ripe, Ripe, I cry,
Full and faire ones; come and buy:
If so be, you ask me where
They doe grow? I answer, There,

Where my *Julia's* lips doe smile;
There's the Land, or Cherry-Ile:
Whose Plantations fully show
All the yeere, where Cherries grow.

DELIGHT IN DISORDER

A SWEET disorder in the dresse
Kindles in cloathes a wantonnesse:
A Lawne about the shoulders thrown
Into a fine distraction:
An erring Lace, which here and there
Enthralls the Crimson Stomacher:
A Cuffe neglectfull, and thereby
Ribbands to flow confusedly:
A winning wave (deserving Note)
In the tempestuous petticote:
A carelesse shooe-string, in whose tye
I see a wilde civility:
Doe more bewitch me, then when Art
Is too precise in every part.

CORINNA'S GOING A MAYING

GET up, get up for shame, the Blooming Morne
Upon her wings presents the god unshorne.
 See how *Aurora* throwes her faire
 Fresh-quilted colours through the aire:
 Get up, sweet-Slug-a-bed, and see
 The Dew-bespangling Herbe and Tree.
Each Flower has wept, and bow'd toward the East,
Above an houre since; yet you not drest,

Nay! not so much as out of bed?
When all the Birds have Mattens seyd,
And sung their thankfull Hymnes: 'tis sin,
Nay, profanation to keep in,
When as a thousand Virgins on this day,
Spring, sooner then the Lark, to fetch in May.

Rise; and put on your Foliage, and be seene
To come forth, like the Spring-time, fresh and
    greene;
And sweet as *Flora*. Take no care
For Jewels for your Gowne, or Haire:
Feare not; the leaves will strew
Gemms in abundance upon you:
Besides, the childhood of the Day has kept,
Against you come, some *Orient Pearls* unwept:
Come, and receive them while the light
Hangs on the Dew-locks of the night:
And *Titan* on the Eastern hill
Retires himselfe, or else stands still
Till you come forth. Wash, dresse, be briefe in
    praying,
Few Beads are best, when once we goe a Maying.

Come, my Corinna, come; and comming, marke
How each field turns a street; each street a Parke
Made green, and trimm'd with trees: see how
Devotion gives each House a Bough,
Or Branch: Each Porch, each doore, ere this,
An Arke a Tabernacle is
Made up of white-thorn neatly enterwove;
As if here were those cooler shades of love.

Can such delights be in the street,
And open fields, and we not see't?
Come, we'll abroad; and let's obay
The Proclamation made for May:
And sin no more, as we have done, by staying;
But my *Corinna*, come, let's goe a Maying.

There's not a budding Boy, or Girle, this day,
But is got up, and gone to bring in May.
   A deale of Youth, ere this, is come
   Back, and with *White-thorn* laden home.
   Some have dispatcht their Cakes and Creame,
   Before that we have left to dreame:
And some have wept, and woo'd, and plighted
      Troth,
And chose their Priest, ere we can cast off sloth:
   Many a green-gown has been given;
   Many a kisse, both odde and even:
   Many a glance too has been sent
   From out the eye, Loves Firmament:
Many a jest told of the Keyes betraying
This night, and Locks pickt, yet w'are not a Maying.

Come, let us goe, while we are in our prime;
And take the harmlesse follie of the time.
   We shall grow old apace, and die
   Before we know our liberty.
   Our life is short; and our dayes run
   As fast away as do's the Sunne:
And as a vapour, or a drop of raine
   Once lost, can ne'r be found againe:
   So when or you or I are made
   A fable, song, or fleeting shade;

ROBERT HERRICK

All love, all liking, all delight
Lies drown'd with us in endlesse night.
Then while time serves, and we are but decaying;
Come, my *Corinna*, come, let's goe a Maying.

LOVE ME LITTLE, LOVE ME LONG

You say, to me-wards your affection's strong;
Pray love me little, so you love me long.
Slowly goes farre: The meane is best: Desire
Grown violent, do's either die, or tire.

UPON JULIA'S CLOTHES

WHEN as in silks my *Julia* goes,
Then, then (me thinks) how sweetly flowes
That liquefaction of her clothes.

Next, when I cast mine eyes and see
That brave Vibration each way free;
O how that glittering taketh me!

ANACR(E)ONTICK VERSE

BRISK methinks I am, and fine,
When I drinke my capring wine:
Then to love I do encline;
When I drinke my wanton wine:
And I wish all maidens mine,
When I drinke my sprightly wine:
Well, I sup, and well I dine,
When I drinke my frolick wine:
But I languish, lowre, and Pine,
When I want my fragrant wine.

THE PILLAR OF FAME

FAMES pillar here, at last, we set,
Out-during *Marble, Brasse,* or *Jet,*
  Charm'd and enchanted so,
    As to withstand the blow
        Of overthrow:
          Nor shall the seas,
          Or OUTRAGES
          Of storms orebear
          What we up-rear,
          Tho Kingdomsfal,
      This pillar never shall
      Decline or waste at all;
But stand for ever by his owne
Firme and well fixt foundation.

To his Book's end this last line he'd have plac't,
Jocond his Muse was; but his Life was chast.

TO FORTUNE

TUMBLE me down, and I will sit
Upon my ruines (smiling yet:)
Teare me to tatters; yet I'le be
Patient in my necessitie.
Laugh at my scraps of cloaths, and shun
Me, as a fear'd infection:
Yet scarre-crow-like I'le walk, as one,
Neglecting thy derision.

THOMAS HEYWOOD
1575—1650

PACK, CLOUDS, AWAY

PACK, clouds, away, and welcome day,
  With night we banish sorrow:
Sweet air blow soft, mount larks aloft
  To give my Love good-morrow!
Wings from the wind to please her mind,—
    Notes from the lark I'll borrow;
Bird, prune thy wing, nightingale, sing!
    To give my Love good-morrow!
      To give my Love good-morrow
      Notes from them both I'll borrow.
Wake from thy nest, Robin-red-breast!
    Sing, birds, in every furrow!
And from each hill, let music shrill
    Give my fair Love good-morrow!
Blackbird and thrush in every bush,
    Stare, linnet, and cock-sparrow,
You pretty elves, amongst yourselves
    Sing my fair Love good-morrow!
      To give my Love good-morrow
      Sing, birds, in every furrow!

HITOMARO
JAPAN

ON PARTING FROM HIS WIFE

NOT yet, O Hill! high hill of Autumn scatter
Red leaves and gold athwart the distant view.
Let me gaze on, a little instant longer,
Where she I love leans toward me through the blue!

HAFIZ

1300—1390

PERSIAN

From the Diwan of Hafiz

VII

FROM the garden of Heaven a western breeze
Blows through the leaves of my garden of earth;
With a love like a huri I'ld take mine ease,
And wine! bring me wine, the giver of mirth!
To-day the beggar may boast him a king,
His banqueting-hall is the ripening field,
And his tent the shadow that soft clouds fling.

A tale of April the meadows unfold—

Ah, foolish for future credit to slave,
And to leave the cash of the present untold!
Build a fort with wine where thy heart may
        brave
The assault of the world; when thy fortress falls,
The relentless victor shall knead from thy dust
The bricks that repair its crumbling walls.

Trust not the word of that foe in the fight!
Shall the lamp of the synagogue lend its flame
To set thy monastic torches alight?
Drunken am I, yet place not my name
In the Book of Doom, nor pass judgment on it;
Who knows what the secret finger of Fate
Upon his own white forehead has writ!

XLII

TRUE love has vanished from every heart:
What has befallen all lovers fair?
When did the bonds of friendship part?—
What has befallen the friends that were?
Ah, why are the feet of Khizr lingering?—
The waters of life are no longer clear,
The purple rose has turned pale with fear,
And what has befallen the wind of Spring?

None now sayeth: "A love was mine,
Loyal and wise, to dispel my care."
None remembers love's right divine:
What has befallen all lovers fair?
In the midst of the field, to the players' feet,
The ball of God's favour and mercy came,
But none has leapt forth to renew the game—
What has befallen the horsemen fleet?

Roses have bloomed, yet no bird rejoiced,
No vibrating throat has rung with the tale;
What can have silenced the hundred-voiced?
What has befallen the nightingale?
Heaven's music is hushed, and the planets roll
In silence; has Zohra broken her lute:
There is none to press out the vine's ripe fruit,
And what has befallen the foaming bowl?

A city where kings are but lovers crowned,
A land from the dust of which friendship springs—
Who has laid waste that enchanted ground?
What has befallen the city of kings?

Years have passed since a ruby was won
From the mine of manhood; they labour in vain,
The fleet-footed wind and the quickening rain,
And what has befallen the light of the sun?

Hafiz, the secret of God's dread task
No man knoweth, in youth or prime
Or in wisest age: of whom would'st thou ask:
What has befallen the wheels of Time?
And when the spirit of Hafiz has fled,
Follow his bier with a tribute of sighs:
Though the ocean of sin has closed o'er his head,
He may find a place in God's Paradise.

Translated by G. L. Bell

CHANG CHI HO
A WORLD APART

THE Lady Moon is my lover,
 My friends are the oceans four,
The heavens have roofed me over,
 And the dawn is my golden door.
I would liefer follow the condor
 Or the seagull, soaring from ken,
Than bury my godhead yonder
 In the dust of the whirl of men.

RALPH HODGSON
1871—

STUPIDITY STREET

I SAW with open eyes
Singing birds sweet
Sold in the shops
For the people to eat,
Sold in the shops of
Stupidity Street.

I saw in vision
The worm in the wheat,
And in the shops nothing
For people to eat;
Nothing for sale in
Stupidity Street.

"TIME, YOU OLD GIPSY MAN"

TIME, you old gipsy man,
Will you not stay,
Put up your caravan
Just for one day?

All things I'll give you
Will you be my guest,
Bells for your jennet
Of silver the best,
Goldsmiths shall beat you
A great golden ring
Peacocks shall bow to you,
Little boys sing,

Oh, and sweet girls will
Festoon you with may.
Time, you old gipsy,
Why hasten away?

Last week in Babylon,
Last night in Rome,
Morning, and in the crush
Under Paul's dome;
Under Paul's dial
You tighten your rein—
Only a moment,
And off once again;
Off to some city
Now blind in the womb,
Off to another
Ere that's in the tomb.

Time, you old gipsy man,
Will you not stay,
Put up your caravan
Just for one day?

JAMES HOGG
1770—1835

THE WITCH OF FIFE

WHERE have ye been, ye ill woman,
    These three lang nights frae hame?
What gars the sweat drap frae yer brow,
    Like drops o' the saut sea-faem?

"It fears me muckle ye have seen
    What gude man never knew;

JAMES HOGG

It fears me muckle ye have been,
  Where the gray cock never crew.

"But the spell may crack, and the bridle break,
  Then sharp yer word will be;
Ye had better sleep in yer bed at hame,
  Wi' yer dear little bairns and me."

"Sit dune, sit dune, my leal auld man,
  Sit dune, and listen to me;
I'll gar the hair stand on yer crown,
  And the cauld sweat blind yer e'e.

"But tell nae words, my gude auld man,
  Tell never a word again;
Or dear shall be your courtesy,
  And driche and sair yer pain.

"The first leet night, when the new moon set,
  When all was douffe and mirk,
We saddled our nags wi' the moonfern leaf,
  And rode frae Kilmerrin kirk.

"Some horses were of the brume-cow framed,
  And some of the green bay tree;
But mine was made of ane hemlock shaw,
  And a stout stallion was he.

"We raide the tod doune on the hill,
  The martin on the law;
And we hunted the owlet out o' breath,
  And forced him doune to fa'."

"What guid was that, ye ill woman?
  What guid was that to thee?
Ye would better have been in yer bed at hame,
  Wi' yer dear little bairns and me."

"And aye we rode, as sae merrily rode,
  Through the merkest gloffs of the night;
And we swam the flood, and we darnit the wood,
  Till we came to the Lommond height.

"And when we came to the Lommond height,
  Sae lightly we lighted doune;
And we drank frae the horns that never grew,
  The beer that was never browin.

"Then up there rose a wee wee man,
  From neath the moss-gray stane;
His face was wan like the colliflower,
  For he neither had blude nor bane.

"He set a reed-pipe till his mouth;
  And he played sae bonnily,
Till the gray curlew, and the blackcock flew
  To listen his melody.

"It rang sae sweet through the green Lommond,
  That the night-wind lowner blew;
And it soupit alang the Loch Leven,
  And wakened the white sea-mew.

"It rang sae sweet through the green Lommond,
  Sae sweetly and sae shrill,
That the weasels leaped out of their mouldy holes,
  And danced on the midnight hill.

"The corby crow came gledging near,
  The erne gaed veering bye;
And the trouts leaped out of the Leven Loch,
  Charmed with the melody.

"And aye we danced on the green Lommond,
  Till the dawn on the ocean grew:
Nae wonder I was a weary wight
  When I cam hame to you."

"What guid, what guid, my weird, weird wyfe,
  What guid was that to thee?
Ye wad better have been in yer bed at hame,
  Wi' yer dear little bairns and me."

"The second night, when the new moon set,
  O'er the roaring sea we flew;
The cockle-shell our trusty bark,
  Our sails of the green sea-rue.

"And the bauld winds blew, and the fire-flauchts
      flew,
  And the sea ran to the sky;
And the thunder it growled, and the sea-dogs howled,
  As we gaed scurrying by.

"And aye we mounted the sea-green hills,
  Till we brushed through the clouds of heaven,
Then soused downright like the stern-shot light,
  Fra the lift's blue casement driven.

"But our tackle stood, and our bark was good,
  And sae pang was our pearly prow;
When we couldna speil the brow of the waves,
  We needled them through below.

"As fast as the hail, as fast as the gale,
  As fast as the midnight leme,
We bored the breast of the bursting swale,
  Or fluffed in the floating faem.

"And when to the Norroway shore we wan,
  We mounted our steeds of the wind,
And we splashed the floode, and we darnit the wood,
  And we left the shore behind.

"Fleet is the roe on the green Lommond,
  And swift is the couryng crew;
The rein-deer dun can eithly run,
  When the hounds and the horns pursue.

"But neither the roe, nor the reindeer dun,
  The hind nor the couryng grew,
Could fly o'er mountain, moor, and dale,
  As our braw steeds they flew.

"The dales were deep, and the Doffrins steep,
  And we rose to the skies ee-bree:
White, white was our road that was never trode,
  O'er the snows of eternity.

"And when we came to the Lapland lone,
  The fairies were all in array,
For all the genii of the north
  Were keeping their holiday.

"The warlock men and the weird women,
  And the fays of the wood and the steep,
And the phantom hunters all were there,
  And the mermaids of the deep.

"And they washed us all with the witch-water,
  Distilled frae the moorland dew,
Till our beauty bloomed like the Lapland rose,
  That wild in the forest grew."

"Ye lee, ye lee, ill woman,
  Sae loud as I hear ye lee!
For the worst-faured wyfe on the shores of Fyfe
  Is comely compared wi' thee."

"Then the mermaids sang, and the woodlands rang,
  Sae sweetly swelled the choir;
On every cliff a harp they hang,
  On every tree a lyre.

"And aye they sang, and the woodlands rang,
  And we drank, and we drank sae deep;
Then soft in the arms of the warlock men,
  We laid us dune to sleep."

"Away, away, ye ill woman,
  And ill death might ye dee!
When ye hae proved sae false to yer God,
  Ye can never prove true to me."

"And there we learned frae the fairy folk,
  And frae our master true,
The words that can bear us through the air,
  And locks and bars undo.

"Last night we met at Maisry's cot;
  Right well the words we knew;
And we set a foot on the black cruik-shell,
  And out at the lum we flew.

"And we flew o'er hill, and we flew o'er dale,
   And we flew o'er firth and sea,
Untill we cam to merry Carlisle,
   Where we lighted on the lea.

"We gaed to the vault beyond the tower,
   Where we entered free as air;
And we drank, and we drank of the bishop's wine
   Till we could drink nae mair."

"Gin that be true, my gude auld wyfe,
   Whilk thou hast tauld to me,
Betide my death, betide my lyfe,
   I'll bear thee company.

"Next time ye gang to merry Carlisle
   To drink of the blude-red wine,
Beshrew my heart, I'll fly with thee,
   If the deil should fly behind."

"Ah, little ye ken, my silly auld man,
   The dangers we maun dree;
Last night we drank of the bishop's wine,
   Till near near taen were we.

"Afore we wan to the sandy ford,
   The gor-cocks nichering flew;
The lofty crest of Ettrick Pen
   Was waved about with blue,
And, flichtering through the air, we fand
   The chill chill morning dew.

"As we flew o'er the hills of Braid,
   The sun rose fair and clear;
There gurly James, and his barons braw,
   Were out to hunt the deer.

"Their bows they drew, their arrows flew,
  And pierced the air with speed,
Till purple fell the morning dew
  With witch-blude rank and red.

"Little ye ken, my silly auld man,
  The dangers we maun dree;
Ne wonder I am a weary wight
  When I come hame to thee."

"But tell me the *word*, my gude auld wyfe,
  Come tell it me speedily;
For I long to drink of the gude red wine,
  And to wing the air with thee.

"Yer hellish horse I willna ride,
  Nor sail the seas in the wind;
But I can flee as well as thee,
  And I'll drink till ye be blind."

"O fy! O fy! my leal auld man,
  That word of darena tell;
It would turn this warld all upside down,
  And make it warse than hell.

"For all the lasses in the land
  Wald mount the wind and fly;
And the men would doff their doublets syde,
  And after them would ply."

But the auld gude man was a cunning auld man,
  And a cunning auld man was he;
And he watched and he watched for mony a night,
  The witches' flight to see.

One night he darnit in Maisry's cot;
   The fearless hags came in;
And he heard the word of awesome weird;
   And he saw their deeds of sin.

Then ane by ane, they said that word,
   As fast to the fire they drew;
Then set a foot on the black cruik-shell,
   And out at the lum they flew.

The auld gudeman came frae his hole
   With fear and muckle dread,
But yet he couldna think to rue,
   For the wine came in his head.

He set his foot in the black cruik-shell,
   With a fixed and a wawling ee;
And he said the word that I darena say,
   And out at the lum flew he.

The witches scaled the moon-beam pale;
   Deep groaned the trembling wind;
But they never wist that our auld gudeman
   Was hovering them behind.

They flew to the vaults of merry Carlisle,
   Where they entered free as air;
And they drank, and they drank of the bishop's wine
   Till they coulde drink nae mair.

The auld gudeman he grew sae crouse,
   He danced on the mouldy ground,
And he sang the bonniest songs of Fife,
   And he tuzzlit the kerlyngs round.

And aye he pierced the tither butt,
  And he sucked, and he sucked sae lang,
Till his een they closed, and his voice grew low,
  And his tongue would hardly gang.

The kerlyngs drank of the bishop's wine
  Till they scented the morning wind;
Then clove again the yielding air,
  And left the auld man behind.

And aye he slept on the damp damp floor,
  He slept and he snored amain;
He never dreamed he was far frae hame,
  Or that the auld wives were gane.

And aye he slept on the damp damp floor,
  Till past the mid-day height,
When wakened by five rough Englishmen,
  That trailed him to the light.

"Now wha are ye, ye silly auld man,
  That sleeps sae sound and sae weel?
How gat ye into the bishop's vault
  Through locks and bars of steel?"

The auld gudeman he tried to speak,
  But ane word he couldna finde;
He tried to think, but his head whirled round,
  And ane thing he couldna minde:

"I cam frae Fyfe," the auld man cried,
  "And I cam on the midnight winde."
They nicked the auld man, and they pricked the auld
    man,

And they yerked his limbs with twine,
Till the red blude ran in his hose and shoon,
But some cried it was wine.

They licked the auld man, and they pricked the auld
man,
And they tyed him till ane stone;
And they set ane bele-fire him about,
To burn him skin and bone.

"O wae to me!" said the puir auld man,
"That ever I saw the day!
And wae be to all the ill women
That lead puir men astray!"

"Let nevir ane auld man after this
To lawless greede incline;
Let never ane auld man after this
Rin post to the deil for wine."

The reeke flew up in the auld man's face,
And choked him bitterlye;
And the low cam up with an angry blaze,
And he singed his auld breek-nee.

He looked to the land frae whence he came,
For looks he could get ne mae;
And he thoughte of his dear little bairns at hame,
And O the auld man was wae!

But they turned their faces to the sun,
With gloffe and wonderous glare,
For they saw ane thing baith large and dun,
Comin sweeping down the air.

That bird it cam frae the lands o' Fife,
   And it cam right tymeouslye,
For who was it but the auld man's wife,
   Just comed his death to see.

She put ane red cap on his head,
   And the auld gudeman looked fain,
Then whispered ane word intil his lug,
   And toved to the aire again.

The auld gudeman he gae ane bob
   I' the midst o' the burning lowe;
And the shackles that bound him to the ring,
   They fell frae his arms like tow.

He drew his breath, and he said the word,
   And he said it with muckle glee,
Then set his feet on the burning pile,
   And away to the air flew he.

Till ance he cleared the swirling reeke,
   He lukit baith feared and sad;
But when he wan to the light blue aire,
   He laughed as he'd been mad.

His arms were spread, and his head was high,
   And his feet stuck out behind;
And the laibies of the auld man's coat
   Were wauffing in the wind.

And aye he neicherit, and aye he flew,
   For he thought the play sae rare;
It was like the voice of the gander blue,
   When he flees through the air.

He lookèd back to the Carlisle men
  As he bored the norlan sky;
He nodded his head, and gave ane girn
  But he never said gude-bye.

They vanished far i' the lift's blue wale,
  Nae maire the English saw,
But the auld man's laugh came on the gale,
  With a lang and a loud guffaw.

May everilke man in the land of Fife
  Read what the drinker's dree;
And never curse his puir auld wife,
  Right wicked although she be.

DANIEL HENRY JUNIOR HOLMES
1851—1908
MARGERY DAW

See-Saw! Margery Daw!
Sold her bed to lie upon straw;
Was she not a dirty slut
To sell her bed, and live in dirt?

AND yet perchance, were the circumstance
But known, of Margery's grim romance
As sacred a veil might cover her then
As the pardon which fell on the Magdalen.

It's a story told so often, so old,
So drearily common, so wearily cold;
A man's adventure—a poor girl's fall—
And a sinless scapegoat born—that's all.

DANIEL HENRY JUNIOR HOLMES

She was simple and young, and the song was sung
With so sweet a voice, in so strange a tongue,
That she follow'd blindly the Devil-song
Till the ground gave way, and she lay headlong.

And then: not a word, not a plea for her heard,
Not a hand held out to the one who had err'd,
Her Christian sisters foremost to condemn—
God pity the woman who falls before them!

They closed the door for evermore
On the contrite heart which repented sore;
And she stood alone, in the outer night,
To feed her baby as best she might.

So she sold her bed, for its daily bread,
The gown off her back, the shawl off her head;
Till her all lay piled on the pawner's shelf,
Then she clench'd her teeth and sold herself.

And so it came that Margery's name
Fell into a burden of Sorrow and Shame;
And Margery's face grew familiar in
The market-place where they trade in sin.

What use to dwell on this premature Hell?
Suffice it to say the child did well,
Till one night that Margery prowled the town,
Sickness was stalking and struck her down.

Her beauty pass'd, and she stood aghast
In the presence of want, and stripped, at the last
Of all she had to be pawned or sold,
To keep her darling from hunger and cold.

So the baby pined, till Margery, blind
With hunger of fever, in body and mind,
At dusk, when Death seem'd close at hand,
Snatch'd a loaf of bread from a baker's stand.

Some Samaritan saw Margery Daw,
And lock'd her in gaol to lie upon straw:
Not a sparrow falls, they say—Oh, well!
God was not looking when Margery fell.

With irons girt, in her felon's shirt,
Poor Margery lies in sorrow and dirt,
A gaunt, sullen woman untimely gray,
With the look of a wild beast brought to bay.

See-saw! Margery Daw!
What a wise and bountiful thing, the Law!
It makes all smooth—for she's out of her head,
And her brat is provided for. It's dead.

OLIVER WENDELL HOLMES
1809—1894

OLD IRONSIDES

Ay, tear her tattered ensign down!
    Long has it waved on high,
And many an eye has danced to see
    That banner in the sky;
Beneath it rung the battle shout,
    And burst the cannon's roar;—
The meteor of the ocean air
    Shall sweep the clouds no more!

Her deck, once red with heroes' blood,
    Where knelt the vanquished foe,
When winds were hurrying o'er the flood,
    And waves were white below,
No more shall feel the victor's tread,
    Or know the conquered knee;—
The harpies of the shore shall pluck
    The eagle of the sea!

O better that her shattered hulk
    Should sink beneath the wave;
Her thunders shook the mighty deep,
    And there should be her grave;
Nail to the mast her holy flag,
    Set every threadbare sail,
And give her to the god of storms,
    The lightning and the gale!

THE WONDERFUL "ONE-HOSS SHAY"

HAVE you heard of the wonderful one-hoss shay,
That was built in such a logical way
It ran a hundred years to a day,
And then, of a sudden, it——ah, but stay,
I'll tell you what happened without delay,
Scaring the parson into fits,
Frightening people out of their wits,—
Have you ever heard of that, I say?

Seventeen hundred and fifty-five.
Georgius Secundus was then alive,—
Snuffy old drone from the German hive.
That was the year when Lisbon-town
Saw the earth open and gulp her down,

And Braddock's army was done so brown,
Left without a scalp to its crown.
It was on the terrible Earthquake-day
That the Deacon finished the one-hoss shay.

Now in building of chaises, I tell you what,
There is always *somewhere* a weakest spot,—
In hub, tire, felloe, in spring or thill,
In panel, or crossbar, or floor, or sill,
In screw, bolt, thoroughbrace,—lurking still,
Find it somewhere you must and will,—
Above or below, or within or without,—
And that's the reason, beyond a doubt,
A chaise *breaks down*, but does n't *wear out*.

But the Deacon swore, (as Deacons do,
With an "I dew vum," or an "I tell *yeou*,")
He would build one shay to beat the taown
'n' the keounty 'n' all the kentry raoun';
It should be so built that it *couldn'* break daown:
—"Fur," said the Deacon, " 't's mighty plain
Thut the weakes' place mus' stan' the strain;
'n' the way t' fix it, uz I maintain,
        Is only jest
T' make that place uz strong uz the rest."

So the Deacon inquired of the village folk
Where he could find the strongest oak,
That couldn't be split nor bent nor broke,—
That was for spokes and floor and sills.
He sent for lancewood to make the thills,
The crossbars were ash from the straightest trees,
The panels of whitewood that cuts like cheese

But lasts like iron for things like these.
The hubs of logs from the "settler's ellum"
Last of its timber—they couldn't sell 'em;
Never an axe had seen their chips
Their blunt ends frizzled like celery-tips;
Step and prop-iron, bolt and screw,
Spring, tire, axle, and linchpin too,
Steel of the finest, bright and blue;
Thoroughbrace bison-skin, thick and wide;
Boot, top, dasher, from tough old hide
Found in the pit when the tanner died.
That was the way he "put her through."—
"There!" said the Deacon, "naow she'll dew!"

Do! I tell you, I rather guess
She was a wonder, and nothing less!
Colts grew horses, beards turned gray,
Deacon and deaconess dropped away,
Children and grandchildren—where were they?
But there stood the stout old one-hoss shay
As fresh as on Lisbon-earthquake-day!

EIGHTEEN HUNDRED;—it came and found
The Deacon's masterpiece strong and sound.
Eighteen hundred increased by ten;—
"Hahnsum kerridge" they called it then.
Eighteen hundred and twenty came;—
Running as usual; much the same.
Thirty and forty at last arrive,
And then came fifty, and FIFTY-FIVE.

Little of all we value here
Wakes on the morn of its hundredth year
Without both feeling and looking queer.

In fact, there's nothing that keeps its youth,
So far as I know, but a tree and truth.
(This is a moral that runs at large;
Take it.—You're welcome.—No extra charge.)

FIRST OF NOVEMBER,—the Earthquake-day—
There are traces of age in the one-hoss shay,
A general flavor of mild decay,
But nothing local, as one may say.
There couldn't be,—for the Deacon's art
Had made it so like in every part
That there wasn't a chance for one to start.
For the wheels were just as strong as the thills,
And the floor was just as strong as the sills,
And the panels just as strong as the floor,
And the whipple-tree neither less nor more,
And the back-crossbar as strong as the fore,
And spring and axle and hub *encore.*
And yet, *as a whole,* it is past a doubt
In another hour it will be *worn out!*

First of November, 'Fifty-five!
This morning the parson takes a drive.
Now, small boys, get out of the way!
Here comes the wonderful one-hoss shay,
Drawn by a rat-tailed, ewe-necked bay.
"Huddup!" said the parson.—Off went they.
The parson was working his Sunday's text,—
Had got to *fifthly,* and stopped perplexed
At what the—Moses—was coming next.
All at once the horse stood still,
Close by the meet'n'-house on the hill.
—First a shiver, and then a thrill,
Then something decidedly like a spill,—

And the parson was sitting upon a rock,
At half past nine by the meet'n'-house clock,—
Just the hour of the Earthquake shock!
—What do you think the parson found,
When he got up and stared around?
The poor old chaise in a heap or mound,
As if it had been to the mill and ground!
You see, of course, if you're not a dunce,
How it went to pieces all at once,—
All at once, and nothing first,—
Just as bubbles do when they burst.

End of the wonderful one-hoss shay.
Logic is logic. That's all I say.

THE LAST LEAF

I saw him once before,
As he passed by the door,
    And again
The pavement stones resound,
As he totters o'er the ground
    With his cane.

They say that in his prime,
Ere the pruning-knife of Time
    Cut him down,
Not a better man was found
By the Crier on his round
    Through the town.

But now he walks the streets
And he looks at all he meets
    Sad and wan,

And he shakes his feeble head,
That it seems as if he said,
  "They are gone."

The mossy marbles rest
On the lips that he has prest
  In their bloom,
And the names he loved to hear
Have been carved for many a year
  On the tomb.

My grandmamma has said,—
Poor old lady, she is dead
  Long ago,—
That he had a Roman nose,
And his cheek was like a rose
  In the snow.

But now his nose is thin,
And it rests upon his chin
  Like a staff,
And a crook is in his back,
And a melancholy crack
  In his laugh.

I know it is a sin
For me to sit and grin
  At him here;
But the old three-cornered hat,
And the breeches, and all that,
  Are so queer!

And if I should live to be
The last leaf upon the tree
  In the spring,—

Let them smile, as I do now,
At the old forsaken bough
    Where I cling.

THE HEIGHT OF THE RIDICULOUS

I WROTE some lines once on a time
    In wondrous merry mood,
And thought, as usual, men would say
    They were exceeding good.

They were so queer, so very queer,
    I laughed as I would die;
Albeit, in the general way,
    A sober man am I.

I called my servant, and he came;
    How kind it was of him
To mind a slender man like me,
    He of the mighty limb!

"These to the printer," I exclaimed,
    And, in my humorous way,
I added, (as a trifling jest,)
    "There 'll be the devil to pay."

He took the paper, and I watched,
    And saw him peep within;
At the first line he read, his face
    Was all upon the grin.

He read the next; the grin grew broad,
    And shot from ear to ear;
He read the third; a chuckling noise
    I now began to hear.

The fourth; he broke into a roar;
    The fifth; his waistband split;
The sixth; he burst five buttons off,
    And tumbled in a fit.

Ten days and nights, with sleepless eye,
    I watched that wretched man,
And since, I never dare to write
    As funny as I can.

CONTENTMENT

"Man wants but little here below."

LITTLE I ask; my wants are few;
    I only wish a hut of stone,
(*A very plain* brown stone will do)
    That I may call my own;—
And close at hand is such a one,
In yonder street that fronts the sun.

Plain food is quite enough for me;
    Three courses are as good as ten;—
If Nature can subsist on three,
    Thank Heaven for three. Amen!
I always thought cold victual nice;—
My *choice* would be vanilla-ice.

I care not much for gold or land;—
    Give me a mortgage here and there,—
Some good bank-stock, some note of hand,
    Or trifling railroad share,—
I only ask that Fortune send
A *little* more than I shall spend.

OLIVER WENDELL HOLMES

Honors are silly toys, I know,
  And titles are but empty names;
I would, *perhaps*, be Plenipo,—
    But only near St. James;
I'm very sure I should not care
To fill our Gubernator's chair.

Jewels are bawbles; 't is a sin
  To care for such unfruitful things;—
One good-sized diamond in a pin,—
    Some, *not so large*, in rings,—
A ruby, and a pearl, or so,
Will do for me;—I laugh at show.

My dame should dress in cheap attire;
  (Good, heavy silks are never dear;)—
I own perhaps I *might* desire
    Some shawls of true Cashmere,—
Some marrowy crapes of China silk,
Like wrinkled skins on scalded milk.

I would not have the horse I drive
  So fast that folks must stop and stare;
An easy gait—two, forty-five—
    Suits me; I do not care;—
Perhaps, for just a *single spurt*,
Some seconds less would do no hurt.

Of pictures, I should like to own
  Titians and Raphaels three or four,—
I love so much their style and tone,—
    One Turner, and no more,
(A landscape,—foreground golden dirt,—
The sunshine painted with a squirt.)

Of books but few,—some fifty score
　For daily use, and bound for wear;
The rest upon an upper floor;—
　　　Some *little* luxury *there*
Of red morocco's gilded gleam,
And vellum rich as country cream.

Busts, cameos, gems,—such things as these,
　Which others often show for pride,
I value for their power to please,
　　　And selfish churls deride;—
One Stradivarius, I confess,
Two Meerschaums, I would fain possess.

Wealth's wasteful tricks I will not learn
　Nor ape glittering upstart fool;—
Shall not carved tables serve my turn,
　　　But *all* must be of buhl?
Give grasping pomp its double share,—
I ask but *one* recumbent chair.

Thus humble let me live and die,
　Nor long for Midas' golden touch;
If Heaven more generous gifts deny,
　　　I shall not miss them *much*,—
Too grateful for the blessing lent
Of simple tastes and mind content!

THE COMET

THE Comet! He is on his way,
　And singing as he flies;
The whizzing planets shrink before
　The spectre of the skies;

OLIVER WENDELL HOLMES

Ah! well may regal orbs burn blue,
 And satellites turn pale,
Ten million cubic miles of head,
 Ten billion leagues of tail!

On, on by whistling spheres of light
 He flashes and he flames;
He turns not to the left nor right,
 He asks them not their names;
One spurn from his demoniac heel,—
 Away, away they fly,
Where darkness might be bottled up
 And sold for "Tyrian dye."

And what would happen to the land,
 And how would look the sea,
If in the bearded devil's path
 Our earth should chance to be?
Full hot and high the sea would boil,
 Full red the forests gleam;
Methought I saw and heard it all
 In a dyspeptic dream!

I saw a tutor take his tube
 The Comet's course to spy;
I heard a scream,—the gathered rays
 Had stewed the tutor's eye;
I saw a fort,—the soldiers all
 Were armed with goggles green;
Popcracked the guns! whiz flew the balls!
 Bang went the magazine!

I saw a poet dip a scroll
　　Each moment in a tub,
I read upon the warping back,
　　"The Dream of Beelzebub";
He could not see his verses burn,
　　Although his brain was fried,
And ever and anon he bent
　　To wet them as they dried.

I saw the scalding pitch roll down
　　The crackling, sweating pines,
And streams of smoke, like water-spouts,
　　Burst through the rumbling mines;
I asked the firemen why they made
　　Such noise about the town;
They answered not,—but all the while
　　The brakes went up and down.

I saw a roasting pullet sit
　　Upon a baking egg;
I saw a cripple scorch his hand
　　Extinguishing his leg;
I saw nice geese upon the wing
　　Towards the frozen pole,
And every mother's gosling fell
　　Crisped to a crackling coal.

I saw the ox that browsed the grass
　　Writhe in the blistering rays,
The herbage in his shrinking jaws
　　Was all a fiery blaze;

I saw huge fishes, boiled to rags,
    Bob through the bubbling brine;
And thoughts of supper crossed my soul;
    I had been rash at mine.

Strange sights! strange sounds! O fearful dream!
    Its memory haunts me still,
The steaming sea, the crimson glare,
    That wreathed each wooded hill;
Stranger! if through thy reeling brain
    Such midnight visions sweep,
Spare, spare, O, spare thine evening meal,
    And sweet shall be thy sleep!

THE CHAMBERED NAUTILUS

THIS is the ship of pearl, which, poets feign,
    Sails the unshadowed main,—
    The venturous bark that flings
On the sweet summer wind its purpled wings
In gulfs enchanted, where the Siren sings,
    And coral reefs lie bare,
Where the cold sea-maids rise to sun their streaming
    hair.

Its webs of living gauze no more unfurl;
    Wrecked is the ship of pearl!
    And every chambered cell,
Where its dim dreaming life was wont to dwell,
As the frail tenant shaped his growing shell,
    Before thee lies revealed,—
Its irised ceiling rent, its sunless crypt unsealed!

Year after year beheld the silent toil
    That spread his lustrous coil;
    Still, as the spiral grew,
He left the past year's dwelling for the new,
Stole with soft step its shining archway through,
    Built up its idle door,
Stretched in his last-found home, and knew the
    old no more.

Thanks for the heavenly message brought by thee,
    Child of the wandering sea,
    Cast from her lap, forlorn!
From thy dead lips a clearer note is born
Than ever Triton blew from wreathéd horn!
    While on mine ear it rings,
Through the deep caves of thought I hear a voice
    that sings:—

Build thee more stately mansions, O my soul,
    As the swift seasons roll!
    Leave thy low-vaulted past!
Let each new temple, nobler than the last,
Shut thee from heaven with a dome more vast,
    Till thou at length art free,
Leaving thine outgrown shell by life's unresting sea!

HOMER

GREECE

900 B.C.

ILIAD

THE DUEL OF PARIS AND MENELAUS

MEANTIME, to beauteous Helen, from the skies
The various goddess of the rainbow flies:
(Like fair Laodicè in form and face,
The loveliest nymph of Priam's royal race:)
Her in the palace, at her loom she found;
The golden web her own sad story crown'd,
The Trojan wars she weaved (herself the prize)
And the dire triumphs of her fatal eyes.
To whom the goddess of the painted bow;
"Approach, and view the wonderous scene below!
Each hardy Greek, and valiant Trojan knight,
So dreadful late, and furious for the fight,
Now rest their spears, or lean upon their shields;
Ceased is the war, and silent all the fields.
Paris alone and Sparta's king advance,
In single fight to toss the beamy lance;
Each met in arms, the fate of combat tries,
Thy love the motive, and thy charms the prize."

This said, the many-colour'd maid inspires
Her husband's love, and wakes her former fires;
Her country, parents, all that once were dear,
Rush to her thought, and force a tender tear.
O'er her fair face a snowy veil she threw,
And, softly sighing, from the loom withdrew.
These, when the Spartan queen approach'd the tower,
In secret own'd resistless beauty's power:

They cried, "No wonder such celestial charms
For nine long years have set the world in arms;
What winning graces! what majestic mien!
She moves a goddess, and she looks a queen!
Yet hence, O Heaven, convey that fatal face,
And from destruction save the Trojan race."
The beauteous warrior now arrays for fight,
In gilded arms magnificently bright:
The purple cuishes clasp his thighs around,
With flowers adorn'd, with silver buckles bound:
Lycaon's corslet his fair body dress'd,
Braced in, and fitted to his softer breast;
A radiant baldric, o'er his shoulder tied,
Sustain'd the sword that glitter'd at his side:
His youthful face a polish'd helm o'erspread;
The waving horse-hair nodded on his head;
His figured shield, a shining orb, he takes,
And in his hand a pointed javelin shakes.
With equal speed, and fired by equal charms,
The Spartan hero sheaths his limbs in arms.

Now round the lists the admiring armies stand,
With javelins fix'd, the Greek and Trojan band.
Amidst the dreadful vale, the chiefs advance,
All pale with rage, and shake the threatening lance.
The Trojan first his shining javelin threw;
Full on Atrides' ringing shield it flew,
Nor pierced the brazen orb, but with a bound
Leap'd from the buckler, blunted, on the ground.
Atrides then his massy lance prepares,
In act to throw, but first prefers his prayers:

"Give me, great Jove! to punish lawless lust,
And lay the Trojan gasping in the dust:
Destroy the aggressor, aid my righteous cause,

Avenge the breach of hospitable laws!
Let this example future times reclaim,
And guard from wrong fair friendship's holy name."
He said, and poised in air the javelin sent,
Through Paris' shield the forceful weapon went,
His corslet pierces, and his garment rends,
And glancing downward, near his flank descends.
The wary Trojan, bending from the blow,
Eludes the death, and disappoints his foe:
But fierce Atrides waved his sword, and strook
Full on his casque; the crested helmet shook;
The brittle steel, unfaithful to his hand,
Broke short; the fragments glitter'd on the sand.
The raging warrior to the spacious skies
Raised his upbraiding voice, and angry eyes:
"Then is it vain in Jove himself to trust?
And is it thus the gods assist the just?
When crimes provoke us, Heaven success denies;
The dart falls harmless, and the falchion flies."
Furious he said, and toward the Grecian crew
(Seized by the crest) the unhappy warrior drew;
Struggling he follow'd, while the embroider'd throng
That tied his helmet, dragg'd the chief along.
Then had his ruin crown'd Atrides' joy,
But Venus trembled for the prince of Troy:
Unseen she came, and burst the golden band;
And left an empty helmet in his hand.
The casque, enraged, amidst the Greeks he threw;
The Greeks with smiles the polish'd trophy view.
Then, as once more he lifts the deadly dart,
In thirst of vengeance, at his rival's heart;
The queen of love her favour'd champion shrouds
(For gods can all things) in a veil of clouds.

Raised from the field of panting youth she led,
And gently laid him on the bridal bed,
With pleasing sweets his fainting sense renews,
And all the dome perfumes with heavenly dews.

Translated by Alexander Pope

DUEL OF HECTOR AND ACHILLES

JOVE lifts the golden balances, that show
The fates of mortal men, and things below:
Here each contending hero's lot he tries,
And weighs, with equal hand, their destinies.
Low sinks the scale surcharged with Hector's fate;
Heavy with death it sinks, and hell receives the
         weight.
  Then Phœbus left him. Fierce Minerva flies
To stern Pelides, and triumphing, cries:
"O loved of Jove! this day our labours cease,
And conquest blazes with full beams on Greece.
Great Hector falls; that Hector famed so far,
Drunk with renown, insatiable of war,
Falls by thy hand, and mine! nor force, nor flight,
Shall more avail him, nor his god of light.
See, where in vain he supplicates above,
Roll'd at the feet of unrelenting Jove;
Rest here: myself will lead the Trojan on,
And urge to meet the fate he cannot shun."
  Her voice divine the chief with joyful mind
Obey'd; and rested, on his lance reclined.
While like Deïphobus the martial dame
(Her face, her gesture, and her arms the same)
In show an aid, by hapless Hector's side
Approach'd, and greets him thus with voice belied:

"Too long, O Hector! have I borne the sight
Of this distress, and sorrow'd in thy flight:
It fits us now a noble stand to make,
And here, as brothers, equal fates partake."

Then he: "O prince! allied in blood and fame,
Dearer than all that own a brother's name;
Of all that Hecuba to Priam bore,
Long tried, long loved: much loved, but honour'd
    more!
Since you, of all our numerous race alone
Defend my life, regardless of your own."

Again the goddess: "Much my father's prayer,
And much my mother's, press'd me to forbear:
My friends embraced my knees, adjured my stay,
But stronger love impell'd, and I obey.
Come then, the glorious conflict let us try,
Let the steel sparkle, and the javelin fly;
Or let us stretch Achilles on the field,
Or to his arm our bloody trophies yield."

Fraudful she said; then swiftly march'd before:
The Dardan hero shuns his foe no more.
Sternly they met. The silence Hector broke;
His dreadful plumage nodded as he spoke:

"Enough, O son of Peleus! Troy has view'd
Her walls thrice circled, and her chief pursued.
But now some god within me bids me try
Thine, or my fate: I kill thee, or I die.
Yet on the verge of battle let us stay,
And for a moment's space suspend the day;
Let heaven's high powers be call'd to arbitrate
The just conditions of this stern debate.
(Eternal witnesses of all below,
And faithful guardians of the treasured vow!)

To them I swear; if, victor in the strife,
Jove by these hands shall shed thy noble life,
No vile dishonour shall thy corse pursue;
Stripp'd of its arms alone (the conqueror's due)
The rest to Greece uninjured I'll restore:
Now plight thy mutual oath, I ask no more."

"Talk not of oaths (the dreadful chief replies,
While anger flash'd from his disdainful eyes)
Detested as thou art, and ought to be,
Nor oath nor pact Achilles plights with thee:
Such pacts, as lambs and rabid wolves combine,
Such leagues, as men and furious lions join,
To such I call the gods! one constant state
Of lasting rancour and eternal hate:
No thought but rage, and never-ceasing strife,
Till death extinguish rage, and thought, and life.
Rouse then thy forces this important hour,
Collect thy soul, and call forth all thy power.
No further subterfuge, no further chance;
'Tis Pallas, Pallas gives thee to my lance.
Each Grecian ghost, by thee deprived of breath,
Now hovers round, and calls thee to thy death."

He spoke, and launch'd his javelin at the foe;
But Hector shunn'd the meditated blow:
He stoop'd, while o'er his head the flying spear
Sang innocent, and spent its force in air.
Minerva watch'd it falling on the land,
Then drew, and gave to great Achilles' hand,
Unseen of Hector, who, elate with joy,
Now shakes his lance, and braves the dread of Troy.

"The life you boasted to that javelin given,
Prince! you have miss'd. My fate depends on heaven.
To thee, presumptuous as thou art, unknown,

Or what must prove my fortune, or thy own.
Boasting is but an art, our fears to blind,
And with false terrors sink another's mind.
But know, whatever fate I am to try,
By no dishonest wound shall Hector die;
I shall not fall a fugitive at least,
My soul shall bravely issue from my breast.
But first, try thou my arm; and may this dart
End all my country's woes, deep buried in thy
    heart!"
  The weapon flew, its course unerring held,
Unerring, but the heavenly shield repell'd,
The mortal dart; resulting with a bound
From off the ringing orb, it struck the ground.
Hector beheld his javelin fall in vain,
Nor other lance, nor other hope remain;
He calls Deïphobus, demands a spear—
In vain, for no Deïphobus was there.
All comfortless he stands: then, with a sigh;
" 'Tis so—heaven wills it, and my hour is nigh!
I deem'd Deïphobus had heard my call,
But he secure lies guarded in the wall.
A god deceived me; Pallas, 'twas thy deed,
Death and black fate approach! 'tis I must bleed.
No refuge now, no succour from above,
Great Jove deserts me, and the son of Jove,
Propitious once, and kind! Then welcome fate!
'Tis true I perish, yet I perish great:
Yet in a mighty deed I shall expire,
Let future ages hear it, and admire!"
  Fierce, at the word, his weighty sword he drew,
And, all collected, on Achilles flew.
So Jove's bold bird, high balanced in the air,

Stoops from the clouds to truss the quivering hare.
Nor less Achilles his fierce soul prepares:
Before his breast the flaming shield he bears,
Refulgent orb! above his fourfold cone
The gilded horse-hair sparkled in the sun,
Nodding at every step: (Vulcanian frame!)
And as he moved, his figure seem'd on flame.
As radiant Hesper shines with keener light,
Far-beaming o'er the silver host of night,
When all the starry train emblaze the sphere:
So shone the point of great Achilles' spear.
In his right hand he waves the weapon round,
Eyes the whole man, and meditates the wound;
But the rich mail Patroclus lately wore,
Securely cased the warrior's body o'er.
One space at length he spies, to let in fate,
Where 'twixt the neck and throat the jointed plate
Gave entrance: through that penetrable part
Furious he drove the well-directed dart:
Nor pierced the windpipe yet, nor took the power
Of speech, unhappy! from thy dying hour.
Prone on the field the bleeding warrior lies,
While, thus triumphing, stern Achilles cries:
    "At last is Hector stretch'd upon the plain,
Who fear'd no vengeance for Patroclus slain:
Then, prince! you should have fear'd, what now you
            feel;
Achilles absent, was Achilles still:
Yet a short space the great avenger staid,
Then low in dust thy strength and glory laid.
Peaceful he sleeps, with all our rites adorn'd,
For ever honour'd, and for ever mourn'd:
While cast to all the rage of hostile power,

Thee, birds shall mangle, and the dogs devour."
 Then Hector, fainting at the approach of death:
"By thy own soul! by those who gave thee breath!
By all the sacred prevalence of prayer;
Ah, leave me not for Grecian dogs to tear!
The common rites of sepulture bestow,
To soothe a father's and a mother's woe;
Let their large gifts procure an urn at least,
And Hector's ashes in his country rest."

 "No, wretch accurst! (relentless he replies;
Flames, as he spoke, shot flashing from his eyes)
Not those who gave me breath should bid me spare,
Nor all the sacred prevalence of prayer.
Could I myself the bloody banquet join!
No—to the dogs that carcase I resign.
Should Troy, to bribe me, bring forth all her store,
And giving thousands, offer thousands more;
Should Dardan Priam, and his weeping dame,
Drain their whole realm to buy one funeral flame:
Their Hector on the pile they should not see,
Nor rob the vultures of one limb of thee."

 Then thus the chief his dying accents drew:
"Thy rage, implacable! too well I knew:
The Furies that relentless breasts have steel'd,
And cursed thee with a heart that cannot yield.
Yet think, a day will come, when fate's decree
And angry gods shall wreak this wrong on thee;
Phœbus and Paris shall avenge my fate,
And stretch thee here, before the Scæan gate."

 He ceased. The fates suppress'd his labouring
   breath,
And his eyes stiffen'd at the hand of death;
To the dark realm the spirit wings its way,

(The manly body left a load of clay)
And plaintive glides along the dreary coast,
A naked, wandering, melancholy ghost!
　　Achilles, musing as he roll'd his eyes
O'er the dead hero, thus unheard, replies:
"Die thou the first! When Jove and heaven ordain,
I follow thee"—He said, and stripp'd the slain.
Then forcing backward from the gaping wound
The reeking javelin, cast it on the ground.
The thronging Greeks behold with wondering eyes
His manly beauty and superior size;
While some, ignobler, the great dead deface
With wounds ungenerous, or with taunts disgrace:
　　"How changed that Hector, who like Jove of late
Sent lightning on our fleets, and scatter'd fate!"
　　High o'er the slain the great Achilles stands,
Begirt with heroes and surrounding bands;
And thus aloud, while all the host attends:
"Princes and leaders! countrymen and friends!
Since now at length the powerful will of heaven
The dire destroyer to our arm has given,
Is not Troy fallen already? Haste, ye powers!
See, if already their deserted towers
Are left unmann'd; or if they yet retain
The souls of heroes, their great Hector slain.
But what is Troy, or glory what to me:
Or why reflects my mind on aught but thee,
Divine Patroclus! Death has seal'd his eyes;
Unwept, unhonour'd, uninterr'd he lies!
Can his dear image from my soul depart,
Long as the vital spirit moves my heart?
If in the melancholy shades below,
The flames of friends and lovers cease to glow,

Yet mine shall sacred last; mine, undecay'd,
Burn on through death, and animate my shade.
Meanwhile, ye sons of Greece, in triumph bring,
The corpse of Hector, and your pæans sing.
Be this the song, slow-moving toward the shore,
"Hector is dead, and Ilion is no more."

    Then his fell soul a thought of vengeance bred
(Unworthy of himself, and of the dead;)
The nervous ancles bored, his feet he bound
With thongs inserted through the double wound;
These fix'd up high behind the rolling wain,
His graceful head was trail'd along the plain.
Proud on his car the insulting victor stood,
And bore aloft his arms, distilling blood.
He smites the steeds; the rapid chariot flies;
The sudden clouds of circling dust arise.
Now lost is all that formidable air;
The face divine, and long-descending hair,
Purple the ground, and streak the sable sand;
Deform'd, dishonour'd, in his native land,
Given to the rage of an insulting throng,
And, in his parents' sight, now dragg'd along!

    The mother first beheld, with sad survey;
She rent her tresses, venerably grey,
And cast, far off, the regal veils away.
With piercing shrieks his bitter fate she moans,
While the sad father answers groans with groans,
Tears after tears his mournful cheeks o'erflow,
And the whole city wears one face of woe:
No less than if the rage of hostile fires,
From her foundations curling to her spires,
O'er the proud citadel at length should rise,
And the last blaze sent Ilion to the skies.

The wretched monarch of the falling state,
Distracted, presses to the Dardan gate.
Scarce the whole people stop his desperate course,
While strong affliction gives the feeble force:
Grief tears his heart, and drives him to and fro,
In all the raging impotence of woe,
At length he roll'd in dust, and thus begun,
Imploring all, and naming one by one:
"Ah! let me, let me go where sorrow calls;
I, only I, will issue from your walls
(Guide or companion, friends! I ask ye none)
And bow before the murderer of my son.
My grief perhaps his pity may engage;
Perhaps at least he may respect my age.
He has a father too; a man like me;
One, not exempt from age and misery
(Vigorous no more, as when his young embrace
Begot this pest of me, and all my race.)
How many valiant sons, in early bloom,
Has that cursed hand sent headlong to the tomb!
Thee, Hector! last: thy loss (divinely brave)
Sinks my sad soul with sorrow to the grave.
O had thy gentle spirit pass'd in peace,
The son expiring in the sire's embrace,
While both thy parents wept the fatal hour,
And, bending o'er thee, mix'd the tender shower!
Some comfort that had been, some sad relief,
To melt in full satiety of grief!"

Thus wail'd the father, groveling on the ground,
And all the eyes of Ilion stream'd around.

Amidst her matrons Hecuba appears,
(A mourning princess, and a train in tears;)
"Ah why has heaven prolong'd this hated breath,

Patient of horrors, to behold thy death?
O Hector! late thy parents' pride and joy,
The boast of nations! the defence of Troy!
To whom her safety and her fame she owed;
Her chief, her hero, and almost her god!
O fatal change! become in one sad day
A senseless corse! inanimated clay!"
   But not as yet the fatal news had spread
To fair Andromache, of Hector dead;
As yet no messenger had told his fate,
Nor e'en his stay without the Scæan gate.
Far in the close recesses of the dome,
Pensive she plied the melancholy loom;
A growing work employ'd her secret hours,
Confusedly gay with intermingled flowers.
Her fair-hair'd handmaids heat the brazen urn,
The bath preparing for her lord's return:
In vain, alas! her lord returns no more!
Unbathed he lies, and bleeds along the shore!
Now from the walls the clamours reach her ear,
And all her members shake with sudden fear;
Forth from her ivory hand the shuttle falls,
And thus, astonish'd, to her maids she calls:

   "Ah follow me! (she cried) what plaintive noise
Invades my ear? 'Tis sure my mother's voice.
My faltering knees their trembling frame desert,
A pulse unusual flutters at my heart;
Some strange disaster, some reverse of fate
 (Ye gods avert it!) threats the Trojan state.
Far be the omen which my thoughts suggest!
But much I fear my Hector's dauntless breast
Confronts Achilles; chased along the plain,
Shut from our walls! I fear, I fear him slain!

Safe in the crowd he ever scorn'd to wait,
And sought for glory in the jaws of fate:
Perhaps that noble heat has cost his breath,
Now quench'd for ever in the arms of death."
 She spoke; and furious, with distracted pace,
Fears in her heart, and anguish in her face,
Flies through the dome (the maids her steps pursue)
And mounts the walls, and sends around her view.
Too soon her eyes the killing object found,
The godlike Hector dragg'd along the ground.
A sudden darkness shades her swimming eyes:
She faints, she falls; her breath, her colour flies.
Her hair's fair ornaments, the braids that bound,
The net that held them, and the wreath that crown'd,
The veil and diadem flew far away
(The gift of Venus on her bridal day.)
Around a train of weeping sisters stands,
To raise her sinking with assistant hands.
Scarce from the verge of death recall'd, again
She faints, or but recovers to complain.
 "O wretched husband of a wretched wife!
Born with one fate, to one unhappy life!
For sure one star its baneful beam display'd
On Priam's roof, and Hippoplacia's shade.
From different parents, different climes we came,
At different periods, yet our fate the same!
Why was my birth to great Aëtion owed,
And why was all that tender care bestow'd?
Would I had never been!—O thou, the ghost
Of my dead husband! miserably lost!
Thou to the dismal realms for ever gone!
And I abandon'd, desolate, alone!
An only child, once comfort of my pains,

Sad product now of hapless love, remains!
No more to smile upon his sire; no friend
To help him now! no father to defend!
For should he 'scape the sword, the common doom,
What wrongs attend him, and what griefs to come!
Even from his own paternal roof expell'd,
Some stranger ploughs his patrimonial field.
The day, that to the shades the father sends,
Robs the sad orphan of his father's friends:
He, wretched outcast of mankind! appears
For ever sad, for ever bathed in tears;
Amongst the happy, unregarded, he
Hangs on the robe, or trembles at the knee,
While those his father's former bounty fed,
Nor reach the goblet, nor divide the bread:
The kindest but his present wants allay,
To leave him wretched the succeeding day.
Frugal compassion! Heedless, they who boast
Both parents still, nor feel what he has lost,
Shall cry, 'Begone! thy father feasts not here:'
The wretch obeys, retiring with a tear.
Thus wretched, thus retiring all in tears,
To my sad soul Astyanax appears!
Forced by repeated insults to return,
And to his widow'd mother vainly mourn:
He, who, with tender delicacy bred,
With princes sported, and on dainties fed,
And when still evening gave him up to rest,
Sunk soft in down upon the nurse's breast,
Must—ah what must he not? Whom Ilion calls
Astyanax, from her well-guarded walls,
Is now that name no more, unhappy boy!
Since now no more thy father guards his Troy.

But thou, my Hector, liest exposed in air,
Far from thy parents' and thy consort's care;
Whose hand in vain, directed by her love,
The martial scarf and robe of triumph wove.
Now to devouring flames be these a prey,
Useless to thee, from this accursed day!
Yet let the sacrifice at least be paid,
An honour to the living, not the dead!"

So spake the mournful dame: her matrons hear
Sigh back her sighs, and answer tear with tear.

Translated by Alexander Pope

THE ODYSSEY

THE SIRENS

'In flowery meads the sportive Sirens play,
Touch the soft lyre, and tune the vocal lay;
Me, me alone, with fetters firmly bound,
The gods allow to hear the dangerous sound.
Hear and obey: if freedom I demand,
Be every fetter strain'd, be added band to band.'

"While yet I speak the winged galley flies,
And lo! the Sirens' shores like mists arise.
Sunk were at once the winds; the air above,
And waves below, at once forgot to move!
Some demon calm'd the air, and smooth'd the deep,
Hush'd the loud winds, and charm'd the waves to
    sleep.
Now every sail we furl, each oar we ply;
Lash'd by the stroke the frothy waters fly.
The ductile wax with busy hands I mould,
And cleft in fragments, and the fragments roll'd;

HOMER

The aërial region now grew warm with day,
The wax dissolved beneath the burning ray;
Then every ear I barr'd against the strain,
And from excess of frenzy lock'd the brain.
Now round the mast my mates the fetters roll'd,
And bound me limb by limb, with fold on fold.
Then bending to the stroke, the active train
Plunge all at once their oars, and cleave the main.

"While to the shore the rapid vessel flies,
Our swift approach the Siren quire descries;
Celestial music warbles from their tongue,
And thus the sweet deluders tune the song:

'O stay, O pride of Greece! Ulysses, stay!
O cease thy course, and listen to our lay!
Bless'd is the man ordain'd our voice to hear,
The song instructs the soul, and charms the ear.
Approach! thy soul shall into raptures rise!
Approach! and learn new wisdom from the wise!
We know whate'er the kings of mighty name
Achieved at Ilion in the field of fame;
Whate'er beneath the sun's bright journey lies,
O stay, and learn new wisdom from the wise!'

"Thus the sweet charmers warbled o'er the main;
My soul takes wing to meet the heavenly strain;
I give the sign, and struggle to be free:
Swift row my mates, and shoot along the sea!
New chains they add, and rapid urge the way,
Till, dying off, the distant sounds decay:
Then scudding swiftly from the dangerous ground,
The deafen'd ear unlock'd, the chains unbound.

Translated by Alexander Pope

ULYSSES' HOMECOMING

THUS, near the gates conferring as they drew,
Argus, the dog, his ancient master knew;
He, not unconscious of the voice and tread,
Lifts to the sound his ear, and rears his head!—
Bred by Ulysses, nourish'd at his board;
But ah! not fated long to please his lord!
To him, his swiftness and his strength were vain;
The voice of glory call'd him o'er the main.
Till then in every sylvan chase renown'd,
With Argus, Argus, rung the woods around;
With him the youth pursued the goat or fawn,
Or traced the mazy leveret o'er the lawn.
Now left to man's ingratitude he lay,
Unhoused, neglected, in the public way;
And where on heaps the rich manure was spread,
Obscene with reptiles, took his sordid bed.

He knew his lord:—he knew, and strove to meet;
In vain he strove to crawl, and kiss his feet;
Yet (all he could) his tail, his ears, his eyes,
Salute his master, and confess his joys.
Soft pity touch'd the mighty master's soul:
Adown his cheek a tear unbidden stole;
Stole unperceived; he turn'd his head, and dried
The drop humane:—then thus impassion'd cried:

"What noble beast in this abandon'd state
Lies here all helpless at Ulysses' gate!
His bulk and beauty speak no vulgar praise;
If, as he seems, he was in better days,
Some care his age deserves: or was he prized
For worthless beauty! therefore now despised?
Such dogs, and men there are; mere things of state,

And always cherish'd by their friends, the great."
  "Not Argus so, (Eumæus thus rejoin'd)
But served a master of a nobler kind:
Who never, never, shall behold him more!
Long, long since perish'd on a distant shore!
O had you seen him, vigorous, bold and young,
Swift as a stag, and as a lion strong!
Him no fell savage on the plain withstood,
None 'scaped him, bosom'd in the gloomy wood;
His eye how piercing, and his scent how true,
To wind the vapour in the tainted dew!
Such, when Ulysses left his natal coast;
Now years unnerve him, and his lord is lost!
The women keep the generous creature bare;
A sleek and idle race is all their care:
The master gone, the servants what restrains?
Or dwells humanity where riot reigns?
Jove fix'd it certain, that whatever day
Makes man a slave, takes half his worth away."
  This said, the honest herdsman strode before:
The musing monarch pauses at the door;
The dog, whom fate had granted to behold
His lord, when twenty tedious years had roll'd,
Takes a last look, and, having seen him, dies;
So closed for ever faithful Argus' eyes!

               Translated by Alexander Pope

THOMAS HOOD
1799—1845

THE BRIDGE OF SIGHS

ONE more unfortunate,
Weary of breath,
Rashly importunate,
Gone to her death!

Take her up tenderly,
Lift her with care;
Fashioned so slenderly,
Young, and so fair!

Look at her garments
Clinging like cerements;
Whilst the wave constantly
Drips from her clothing;
Take her up instantly,
Loving, not loathing.—

Touch her not scornfully;
Think of her mournfully,
Gently and humanly;
Not of the stains of her,
All that remains of her
Now is pure womanly.

Make no deep scrutiny
Into her mutiny
Rash and undutiful:
Past all dishonor,
Death has left on her
Only the beautiful.

Still, for all slips of hers,
One of Eve's family—
Wipe those poor lips of hers
Oozing so clammily.

Loop up her tresses
Escaped from the comb,
Her fair auburn tresses;
Whilst wonderment guesses
Where was her home?

Who was her father?
Who was her mother?
Had she a sister?
Had she a brother?
Or was there a dearer one
Still, and a nearer one
Yet, than all other?

Alas for the rarity
Of Christian charity
Under the sun!
O, it was pitiful!
Near a whole city full,
Home she had none.

Sisterly, brotherly,
Fatherly, motherly
Feelings had changed:
Love, by harsh evidence,
Thrown from its eminence;
Even God's providence
Seeming estranged.

Where the lamps quiver
So far in the river,
With many a light
From window and casement,
From garret to basement,
She stood, with amazement,
Houseless by night.

The bleak wind of March
Made her tremble and shiver;
But not the dark arch,
Or the black flowing river:
Mad from life's history,
Glad to death's mystery,
Swift to be hurled—
Anywhere, anywhere
Out of the world!

In she plunged boldly,
No matter how coldly
The rough river ran,—
Over the brink of it,
Picture it—think of it
Dissolute man!
Lave in it, drink of it.
Then, if you can!

Take her up tenderly,
Lift her with care;
Fashioned so slenderly,
Young, and so fair!

Ere her limbs frigidly
Stiffen too rigidly,

Decently,—kindly,—
Smooth, and compose them;
And her eyes, close them,
Staring so blindly!

Dreadfully staring
Through muddy impurity,
As when with the daring
Last look of despairing
Fixed on futurity.

Perishing gloomily,
Spurred by contumely,
Cold inhumanity,
Burning insanity,
Into her rest.—
Cross her hands humbly,
As if praying dumbly,
Over her breast!

Owning her weakness,
Her evil behavior,
And leaving, with meekness,
Her sins to her Saviour!

THE SONG OF THE SHIRT

WITH fingers weary and worn,
  With eyelids heavy and red,
A woman sat in unwomanly rags,
  Plying her needle and thread—
    Stitch! stitch! stitch!
In poverty, hunger, and dirt,
  And still with a voice of dolorous pitch
She sang the "Song of the Shirt!"

"Work! work! work!
While the cock is crowing aloof!
    And work—work—work,
Till the stars shine through the roof.
It's O! to be a slave
    Along with the barbarous Turk,
Where woman has never a soul to save,
    If this is Christian work!

    "Work—work—work
Till the brain begins to swim!
    Work—work—work
Till the eyes are heavy and dim!
Seams, and gusset, and band,
    Band, and gusset, and seam,
Till over the buttons I fall asleep,
    And sew them on in a dream!

"O, men, with sisters dear!
    O, men, with mothers and wives!
It is not linen you're wearing out,
    But human creatures' lives!
        Stitch—stitch—stitch,
    In poverty, hunger, and dirt,
Sewing at once, with a double thread,
    A shroud as well as a shirt.

"But why do I talk of death?
    That phantom of grisly bone,
I hardly fear his terrible shape,
    It seems so like my own—
It seems so like my own,
    Because of the fasts I keep;

O, God! that bread should be so dear.
And flesh and blood so cheap!

"Work—work—work!
    My labor never flags;
And what are its wages? A bed of straw,
    A crust of bread—and rags.
That shattered roof—and this naked floor—
    A table—a broken chair—
And a wall so blank, my shadow I thank
    For sometimes falling there!

"Work—work—work!
    From weary chime to chime,
Work—work—work,
    As prisoners work for crime!
Band, and gusset, and seam,
    Seam, and gusset, and band,
Till the heart is sick, and the brain benumbed,
    As well as the weary hand.

    "Work—work—work,
In the dull December light,
    And work—work—work,
When the weather is warm and bright—
While underneath the eaves
    The brooding swallows cling,
As if to show me their sunny backs,
    And twit me with the spring.

    "O! but to breathe the breath
Of the cowslip and primrose sweet—
    With the sky above my head,
And the grass beneath my feet,

For only one short hour
    To feel as I used to feel,
Before I knew the woes of want,
    And the walk that costs a meal!

"O! but for one short hour!
    A respite however brief!
No blessed leisure for love or hope,
    But only time for grief!
A little weeping would ease my heart,
    But in their briny bed
My tears must stop, for every drop
    Hinders needle and thread!"

With fingers weary and worn,
    With eyelids heavy and red,
A woman sat in unwomanly rags,
    Plying her needle and thread—
      Stitch! stitch! stitch!
    In poverty, hunger, and dirt,
And still with a voice of dolorous pitch,—
Would that its tone could reach the rich!—
    She sang this "Song of the Shirt!"

FAIR INES

O saw ye not fair Ines?
She's gone into the west,
To dazzle when the sun is down,
And rob the world of rest:
She took our daylight with her,
The smiles that we love best,
With morning blushes on her cheek,
And pearls upon her breast.

O turn again, fair Ines,
Before the fall of night,
For fear the moon should shine alone,
And stars unrivalled bright;
And blessed will the lover be
That walks beneath their light,
And breathes the love against thy cheek
I dare not even write!

Would I had been, fair Ines,
That gallant cavalier,
Who rode so gayly by thy side,
And whispered thee so near!—
Where there no bonny dames at home,
Or no true lovers here,
That he should cross the seas to win
The dearest of the dear?

I saw thee, lovely Ines,
Descend along the shore,
With bands of noble gentlemen,
And banners waved before:
And gentle youth and maidens gay,
And snowy plumes they wore;—
It would have been a beauteous dream,
—If it had been no more!

Alas, alas! fair Ines,
She went away with song,
With music waiting on her steps,
And shoutings of the throng;
But some were sad, and felt no mirth,
But only music's wrong,
In sounds that sang farewell, farewell,
To her you've loved so long.

Farewell, farewell, fair Ines!
That vessel never bore
So fair a lady on its deck,
Nor danced so light before,—
Alas for pleasure on the sea,
And sorrow on the shore!
The smile that blest one lover's heart
Has broken many more.

THE DREAM OF EUGENE ARAM

'T was in the prime of summer time,
    An evening calm and cool,
And four-and-twenty happy boys
    Came bounding out of school:
There were some that ran, and some that leapt,
    Like troutlets in a pool.

Away they sped with gamesome minds,
    And souls untouched by sin;
To a level mead they came, and there
    They drave the wickets in:
Pleasantly shone the setting sun
    Over the town of Lynn.

Like sportive deer they coursed about,
    And shouted as they ran,—
Turning to mirth all things of earth,
    As only boyhood can;
But the Usher sat remote from all,
    A melancholy man!

His hat was off, his vest apart,
    To catch heaven's blessed breeze;

For a burning thought was in his brow,
      And his bosom ill at ease:
So he leaned his head on his hands, and read
      The book between his knees!

Leaf after leaf he turned it o'er,
      Nor ever glanced aside,
For the peace of his soul he read that book
      In the golden eventide:
Much study had made him very lean,
      And pale, and leaden-eyed.

At last he shut the ponderous tome,
      With a fast and fervent grasp
He strained the dusky covers close,
      And fixed the brazen hasp:
"O, God! could I so close my mind,
      And clasp it with a clasp!"

Then leaping on his feet upright,
      Some moody turns he took,—
Now up the mead, then down the mead,
      And past a shady nook,—
And, lo! he saw a little boy
      That pored upon a book!

"My gentle lad, what is 't you read—
      Romance or fairy fable?
Or is it some historic page,
      Of kings and crowns unstable?"
The young boy gave an upward glance,—
      "It is 'The Death of Abel.' "

The Usher took six hasty strides,
    As smit with sudden pain,—
Six hasty strides beyond the place,
    Then slowly back again;
And down he sat beside the lad,
    And talked with him of Cain;

And, long since then, of bloody men,
    Whose deeds tradition saves;
Of lonely folk cut off unseen,
    And hid in sudden graves;
Of horrid stabs in groves forlorn,
    And murders done in caves;

And how the sprites of injured men
    Shriek upward from the sod,—
Ay, how the ghostly hand will point
    To show the burial clod;
And unknown facts of guilty acts
    Are seen in dreams from God!

He told how murderers walk the earth
    Beneath the curse of Cain,—
With crimson clouds before their eyes,
    And flames about their brain:
For blood has left upon their souls
    Its everlasting stain!

"And well," quoth he, "I know, for truth,
    Their pangs must be extreme,—
Woe, woe, unutterable woe,—
    Who spill life's sacred stream!
For why? Methought, last night, I wrought
    A murder, in a dream!

"One that had never done me wrong—
　　A feeble man and old;
I led him to a lonely field,—
　　The moon shone clear and cold:
Now here, said I, this man shall die
　　And I will have his gold!

"Two sudden blows with a ragged stick,
　　And one with a heavy stone,
One hurried gash with a hasty knife,—
　　And then the deed was done:
There was nothing lying at my foot
　　But lifeless flesh and bone!

"Nothing but lifeless flesh and bone,
　　That could not do me ill;
And yet I feared him all the more,
　　For lying there so still:
There was a manhood in his look,
　　That murder could not kill!

"And, lo! the universal air
　　Seemed lit with ghastly flame;—
Ten thousand thousand dreadful eyes
　　Were looking down in blame:
I took the dead man by his hand,
　　And called upon his name!

"O, God! it made me quake to see
　　Such sense within the slain!
But when I touched the lifeless clay,
　　The blood gushed out amain!
For every clot, a burning spot
　　Was scorching in my brain!

"My head was like an ardent coal,
    My heart as solid ice;
My wretched, wretched soul, I knew,
    Was at the devil's price:
A dozen times I groaned; the dead
    Had never groaned but twice!

"And now, from forth the frowning sky,
    From the heaven's topmost height,
I heard a voice—the awful voice
    Of the blood-avenging sprite:—
"Thou guilty man! take up thy dead
    And hide it from my sight!"

"I took the dreary body up,
    And cast it in a stream,—
A sluggish water, black as ink,
    The depth was so extreme:—
My gentle Boy, remember this
    Is nothing but a dream!

"Down went the corse with a hollow plunge,
    And vanished in the pool;
Anon I cleansed my bloody hands,
    And washed my forehead cool,
And sat among the urchins young,
    That evening, in the school.

"O, Heaven! to think of their white souls,
    And mine so black and grim!
I could not share in childish prayer,
    Nor join in evening hymn:
Like a devil of the pit I seemed,
    'Mid holy cherubim!

"And peace went with them, one and all,
 And each calm pillow spread;
But Guilt was my grim chamberlain
 That lighted me to bed;
And drew my midnight curtains round,
 With fingers bloody red!

"All night I lay in agony,
 In anguish dark and deep;
My fevered eyes I dared not close,
 But stared aghast at Sleep:
For Sin had rendered unto her
 The keys of hell to keep!

"All night I lay in agony,
 From weary chime to chime,
With one besetting horrid hint
 That racked me all the time;
A mighty yearning, like the first
 Fierce impulse unto crime!

"One stern tyrannic thought, that made
 All other thoughts its slave;
Stronger and stronger every pulse
 Did that temptation crave,—
Still urging me to go and see
 The Dead Man in his grave!

"Heavily I rose up, as soon
 As light was in the sky,
And sought the black accursèd pool
 With a wild misgiving eye;
And I saw the Dead in the river bed,
 For the faithless stream was dry.

"Merrily rose the lark, and shook
    The dew-drop from its wing;
But I never marked its morning flight,
    I never heard it sing:
For I was stooping once again
    Under the horrid thing.

"With breathless speed, like a soul in chase,
    I took him up and ran;—
There was no time to dig a grave
    Before the day began:
In a lonesome wood, with heaps of leaves,
    I hid the murdered man!

"And all that day I read in school,
    But my thought was other where;
As soon as the mid-day task was done,
    In secret I was there:
And a mighty wind had swept the leaves,
    And still the corse was bare!

"Then down I cast me on my face,
    And first began to weep,
For I knew my secret then was one
    That earth refused to keep:
Or land or sea, though he should be
    Ten thousand fathoms deep.

"So wills the fierce avenging Sprite,
    Till blood for blood atones!
Ay, though he's buried in a cave,
    And trodden down with stones,
And years have rotted off his flesh,—
    The world shall see his bones!

"O, God! that horrid, horrid dream
 Besets me now awake!
Again—again, with dizzy brain,
 The human life I take;
And my red hand grows raging hot,
 Like Cranmer's at the stake

"And still no peace for the restless clay
 Will wave or mould allow;
The horrid thing pursues my soul,—
 It stands before me now!"
The fearful Boy looked up, and saw
 Huge drops upon his brow.

That very night, while gentle sleep
 The urchin eyelids kissed,
Two stern-faced men set out from Lynn,
Through the cold and heavy mist:
And Eugene Aram walked between,
 With gyves upon his wrist.

RUTH

SHE stood breast-high amid the corn,
Clasped by the golden light of morn,
 Like the sweetheart of the sun,
 Who many a glowing kiss had won.

On her cheek an autumn flush,
Deeply ripened;—such a blush
 In the midst of brown was born,
 Like red poppies grown with corn.

Round her eyes her tresses fell;
Which were blackest none could tell,
But long lashes veiled a light
That had else been all too bright.

And her hat, with shady brim,
Made her tressy forehead dim;—
Thus she stood amid the stooks,
Praising God with sweetest looks:—

Sure, I said, Heaven did not mean
Where I reap thou shouldst but glean;
Lay thy sheaf adown and come,
Share my harvest and my home.

I REMEMBER, I REMEMBER

I REMEMBER, I remember
The house where I was born,
The little window where the sun
Came peeping in at morn;
He never came a wink too soon,
Nor brought too long a day;
But now I often wish the night
Had borne my breath away!

I remember, I remember
The roses red and white,
The violets, and the lily-cups,
Those flowers made of light!
The lilacs where the robin built,
And where my brother set
The laburnum on his birth-day,—
The tree is living yet!

THOMAS HOOD

I remember, I remember
Where I was used to swing,
And thought the air must rush as fresh
To swallows on the wing;
My spirit flew in feathers then,
That is so heavy now,
And summer pools could hardly cool
The fever on my brow!

I remember, I remember
The fir-trees dark and high;
I used to think their slender tops
Were close against the sky:
It was a childish ignorance,
But now 'tis little joy
To know I'm further off from heaven
Than when I was a boy.

GOLD

Gold! gold! gold! gold!
Bright and yellow, hard and cold,
Molten, graven, hammered and rolled;
Heavy to get, and light to hold;
Hoarded, bartered, bought, and sold,
Stolen, borrowed, squandered, doled:
Spurned by the young, but hugged by the old
To the very verge of the church-yard mould;
Price of many a crime untold:
Gold! gold! gold! gold!
Good or bad a thousand-fold!
  How widely its agencies vary—

To save—to ruin—to curse—to bless—
As even its minted coins express,
Now stamped with the image of good Queen Bess,
  And now of a Bloody Mary.

FAITHLESS NELLY GRAY

BEN BATTLE was a soldier bold,
    And used to war's alarms;
But a cannon-ball took off his legs,
    So he laid down his arms!

Now, as they bore him off the field,
    Said he, "Let others shoot,
For here I leave my second leg,
    And the Forty-second Foot!"

The army-surgeons made him limbs:
    Said he, "They're only pegs:
But there's as wooden members quite
    As represent my legs!"

Now, Ben he loved a pretty maid,
    Her name was Nelly Gray;
So he went to pay her his devours,
    When he devoured his pay!

But when he called on Nelly Gray,
    She made him quite a scoff;
And when she saw his wooden legs,
    Began to take them off!

"O, Nelly Gray! O, Nelly Gray
    Is this your love so warm?

The love that loves a scarlet coat
  Should be more uniform!"

Said she, "I loved a soldier once
  For he was blithe and brave;
But I will never have a man
  With both legs in the grave!

"Before you had those timber toes,
  Your love I did allow,
But then, you know, you stand upon
  Another footing now!"

"O, Nelly Gray! O, Nelly Gray!
  For all your jeering speeches,
At duty's call, I left my legs,
  In Badajos's *breaches!*"

"Why then," said she, "you've lost the feet
  Of legs in war's alarms,
And now you cannot wear your shoes
  Upon your feats of arms!"

"O, false and fickle Nelly Gray!
  I know why you refuse:—
Though I've no feet—some other man
  Is standing in my shoes!

"I wish I ne'er had seen your face;
  But, now, a long farewell!
For you will be my death;—alas
  You will not be my *Nell!*"

Now, when he went from Nelly Gray,
    His heart so heavy got,
And life was such a burthen grown,
    It made him take a knot!

So round his melancholy neck
    A rope he did entwine,
And, for his second time in life,
    Enlisted in the Line!

One end he tied around a beam,
    And then removed his pegs,
And, as his legs were off,—of course,
    He soon was off his legs!

And there he hung, till he was dead
    As any nail in town,—
For, though distress had cut him up,
    It could not cut him down!

A dozen men sat on his corpse,
    To find out why he died—
And they buried Ben in four cross-roads,
    With a *stake* in his inside!

LAURENCE HOPE
1865—1904

VALGOVIND'S SONG IN THE SPRING

THE Temple bells are ringing,
The young green corn is springing,
        And the marriage month is drawing very
                                                near.

LAURENCE HOPE

I lie hidden in the grass,
And I count the moments pass,
  For the month of marriages is drawing near.

Soon, ah, soon, the women spread
The appointed bridal bed
  With hibiscus buds and crimson marriage
               flowers,

Where, when all the songs are done,
And the dear dark night begun,
  I shall hold her in my happy arms for hours.

She is young and very sweet,
From the silver on her feet
  To the silver and the flowers in her hair,

And her beauty makes me swoon,
As the Moghra trees at noon
  Intoxicate the hot and quivering air.

Ah, I would the hours were fleet
As her silver-circled feet,
  I am weary of the daytime and the night.

I am weary unto death,
Oh, my rose with jasmine breath
  With this longing for your beauty and your
               light.

KASHMIRI SONG

PALE hands I love beside the Shalimar,
 Where are you now? Who lies beneath your spell?
Whom do you lead on Rapture's roadway, far,
 Before you agonise them in farewell?

Oh, pale dispensers of my Joys and Pains,
   Holding the doors of Heaven and of Hell,
How the hot blood rushed wildly through the veins
   Beneath your touch, until you waved farewell.

Pale hands, pink tipped, like Lotus buds that float
   On those cool waters where we used to dwell,
I would have rather felt you round my throat,
   Crushing out life, than waving me farewell!

"LESS THAN THE DUST"

Less than the dust, beneath thy Chariot wheel,
Less than the rust, that never stained thy Sword,
Less than the trust thou hast in me, O Lord,
                  Even less than these!

Less than the weed, that grows beside thy door,
Less than the speed of hours spent far from thee,
Less than the need thou hast in life of me,
                  Even less am I.

Since I, O Lord, am nothing unto thee,
See here thy Sword, I make it keen and bright,
Love's last reward, Death comes to me to-night,
                 Farewell,   Zahir-u-din.

HORACE
LATIN
65—8 B.C.

TO CHLORIS

HORACE: BOOK III, ODE 15.
"Uxor paupers Ibyci—"

YOUR conduct, naughty Chloris, is
Not just exactly Horace's
   Ideal of a lady
   At the shady
      Time of life;
You mustn't throw your soul away
On foolishness, like Pholoë—
   Her days are folly-laden—
   She's a maiden,
      You're a wife.

Your daughter, with propriety,
May look for male society,
   Do one thing and another
   In which mother
      Shouldn't mix;
But revels Bacchanalian
Are—or should be—quite alien
   To you a married person,
   Something worse'n
      Forty-six!

Yes, Chloris, you cut up too much,
You love the dance and cup too much.

Your years are quickly flitting,
  To your knitting
    Right about!
Forget the incidental things
That keep you from parental things,
  The World, the Flesh, the Devil,
  On the level
    Cut 'em out!

Translated by F. P. Adams

TO PYRRHA

HORACE: BOOK I, ODE 5

"Quis multa gracilis te puer in rosa"

What lady-like youth in his wild aberrations
  Is putting cologne on his brow?
For whom are the puffs and the blond transforma-
      tions?
  I wonder who's kissing you now.*

Tee hee! I must laugh when I think of his finish,
  Not wise to your ways and your rep.
Ha! ha! how his fancy for you will diminish!
  I know, for I'm Jonathan Hep.

Translated by F. P. Adams

* Paraphraser's note: Horace beat the modern song writers to
this. The translation is literal enough—"Quis . . . gracilis te
puer . . . urget?"

"PERSICOS ODI"

DAVUS, I detest
  Orient display;
Wreaths on linden drest,
Davus, I detest.
Let the late rose rest
  Where it fades away:—
Davus, I detest
  Orient display.

Naught but myrtle twine
  Therefore, Boy, for me,
Sitting 'neath the vine,—
Naught but myrtle twine;
Fitting to the wine,
  Not unfitting thee;
Naught but myrtle twine
  Therefore, Boy, for me.

Translated by Austin Dobson

"VITAS HINNULEO"

You shun me, Chloe, wild and shy
  As some stray fawn that seeks its mother
Through trackless woods. If spring-winds sigh,
  It vainly strives its fears to smother;—

Its trembling knees assail each other
  When lizards stir the bramble dry;—
  You shun me, Chloe, wild and shy
As some stray fawn that seeks its mother.

And yet no Libyan lion I,—
　No ravening thing to rend another;
Lay by your tears, your tremors by—
　A Husband's better than a brother;
Nor shun me, Chloe, wild and shy
　As some stray fawn that seeks its mother.

Translated by Austin Dobson

RICHARD HENGUIST HORNE
1803—1884

PELTERS OF PYRAMIDS

A SHOAL of idlers, from a merchant craft
Anchor'd off Alexandria, went ashore,
And mounting asses in their headlong glee,
Round Pompey's Pillar rode with hoots and taunts,
As men oft say, "What art thou more than we?"
Next in a boat they floated up the Nile,
Singing and drinking, swearing senseless oaths,
Shouting, and laughing most derisively
At all majestic scenes. A bank they reach'd,
And clambering up, play'd gambols among tombs;
And in portentous ruins (through whose depths,
The mighty twilight of departed Gods,
Both sun and moon glanced furtive, as in awe)
They hid, and whoop'd, and spat on sacred things.

At length, beneath the blazing sun they lounged
Near a great Pyramid. Awhile they stood
With stupid stare, until resentment grew,
In the recoil of meanness from the vast;
And gathering stones, they with coarse oaths and
　　jibes

(As they would say, "What art thou more than
    we?")
Pelted the Pyramid! But soon these men,
Hot and exhausted, sat them down to drink—
Wrangled, smok'd, spat, and laugh'd, and drowsily
Curs'd the bald Pyramid, and fell asleep.

Night came:—a little sand went drifting
    by—
And morn again was in the soft blue heavens.
The broad slopes of the shining Pyramid
Look'd down in their austere simplicity
Upon the glistening silence of the sands
Whereon no trace of mortal dust was seen.

A. E. HOUSMAN

1859—

WHEN I WAS ONE AND TWENTY

When I was one-and-twenty
    I heard a wise man say,
'Give crowns and pounds and guineas
    But not your heart away;
Give pearls away and rubies
    But keep your fancy free.'
But I was one-and-twenty,
    No use to talk to me.

When I was one-and-twenty
    I heard him say again,
'The heart out of the bosom
    Was never given in vain;

'Tis paid with sighs a plenty
   And sold for endless rue.'
And I am two-and-twenty,
   And oh, 'tis true, 'tis true.

MYSELF AGAIN

OH, when I was in love with you,
   Then I was clean and brave,
And miles around the wonder grew
   How well did I behave.

And now the fancy passes by,
   And nothing will remain,
And miles around they'll say that I
   Am quite myself again.

WITH RUE MY HEART IS LADEN

WITH rue my heart is laden
   For golden friends I had,
For many a rose-lipt maiden
   And many a lightfoot lad.

By brooks too broad for leaping
   The lightfoot boys are laid;
The rose-lipt girls are sleeping
   In fields where roses fade.

MITHRIDATES

'TERENCE, this is stupid stuff:
You eat your victuals fast enough;
There can't be much amiss, 'tis clear,
To see the rate you drink your beer.

But oh, good Lord, the verse you make,
It gives a chap the belly-ache.
The cow, the old cow, she is dead;
It sleeps well, the hornèd head:
We poor lads, 'tis our turn now
To hear such tunes as killed the cow.
Pretty friendship 'tis to rhyme
Your friends to death before their time
Moping melancholy mad:
Come, pipe a tune to dance to, lad.'

Why, if 'tis dancing you would be,
There's brisker pipes than poetry.
Say, for what were hop-yards meant,
Or why was Burton built on Trent?
Oh, many a peer of England brews
Livelier liquor than the Muse,
And malt does more than Milton can
To justify God's ways to man.
Ale, man, ale's the stuff to drink
For fellows whom it hurts to think:
Look into the pewter pot
To see the world as the world's not.
And faith, 'tis pleasant till 'tis past:
The mischief is that 'twill not last.
Oh I have been to Ludlow fair
And left my necktie God knows where,
And carried half way home, or near,
Pints and quarts of Ludlow beer:
Then the world seemed none so bad,
And I myself a sterling lad;
And down in lovely muck I've lain,
Happy till I woke again.

Then I saw the morning sky:
Heigho, the tale was all a lie;
The world, it was the old world yet,
I was I, my things were wet,
And nothing now remained to do
But begin the game anew.

Therefore, since the world has still
Much good, but much less good than ill,
And while the sun and moon endure
Luck's a chance, but trouble's sure,
I'd face it as a wise man would,
And train for ill and not for good.
'Tis true, the stuff I bring for sale
Is not so brisk a brew as ale:
Out of a stem that scored the hand
I wrung it in a weary land.
But take it: if the smack is sour,
The better for the embittered hour;
It should do good to heart and head
When your soul is in my soul's stead;
And I will friend you, if I may
In the dark and cloudy day.

There was a king reigned in the East:
There, when kings will sit to feast,
They get their fill before they think
With poisoned meat and poisoned drink.
He gathered all that springs to birth
From the many-venomed earth;
First a little, thence to more,
He sampled all her killing store;
And easy, smiling, seasoned sound,

Sate the king when healths went round.
They put arsenic in his meat
And stared aghast to watch him eat;
They poured strychnine in his cup
And shook to see him drink it up:
They shook, they stared as white's their shirts.
Them it was their poison hurt.
—I tell the tale that I heard told.
Mithridates, he died old.

RICHARD HOVEY
1864—1900
THE SEA GIPSY

I AM fevered with the sunset,
I am fretful with the bay,
For the wander-thirst is on me
And my soul is in Cathay.

There's a schooner in the offing,
With her topsails shot with fire,
And my heart has gone aboard her
For the Islands of Desire.

I must forth again to-morrow!
With the sunset I must be
Hull down on the trail of rapture
In the wonder of the sea.

A STEIN SONG.

GIVE a rouse, then, in the Maytime
For a life that knows no fear!
Turn night-time into daytime
With the sunlight of good cheer!
For it's always fair weather
When good fellows get together,
With a stein on the table and a good song ringing
    clear.

When the wind comes up from Cuba
And the birds are on the wing,
And our hearts are patting juba
To the banjo of the spring,
Then it's no wonder whether
The boys will get together,
With a stein on the table and a cheer for everything.

For we're all frank-and-twenty
When the spring is in the air;
And we've faith and hope a-plenty,
And we've life and love to spare;
And it's birds of a feather
When we all get together,
With a stein on the table and a heart without a care.

For we know the world is glorious,
And the goal a golden thing,
And that God is not censorious
When his children have their fling;
And life slips its tether
When the boys get together,
With a stein on the table in the fellowship of spring.

BARNEY McGEE

BARNEY McGEE, there's no end of good luck in you,
Will-o'-the-wisp, with a flicker of Puck in you,
Wild as a bull-pup, and all of his pluck in you—
Let a man tread on your coat and he'll see!
Eyes like the lakes of Killarney for clarity,
Nose that turns up without any vulgarity,
Smile like a cherub, and hair that is carroty—
Whoop, you're a rarity, Barney McGee!
Mellow as Tarragon,
Prouder than Aragon—
Hardly a paragon,
You will agree—
Here's all that's fine to you!
Books and old wine to you!
Girls be divine to you,
Barney McGee!

Lucky the day when I met you unwittingly,
Dining where vagabonds came and went flittingly.
Here's some *Barbera* to drink it befittingly,
That day at Silvio's, Barney McGee!
Many's the time we have quaffed our Chianti there,
Listened to Silvio quoting us Dante there—
Once more to drink Nebiolo Spumante there,
How we'd pitch Pommery into the sea!
There where the gang of us
Met ere Rome rang of us,
They had the hang of us
To a degree.
How they would trust to you!
That was but just to you.

Here's o'er their dust to you,
Barney McGee!

Barney McGee, when you're sober you scintillate,
But when you're in drink you're the pride of the in-
       tellect;
Divil a one of us ever came in till late.
Once at the bar where you happened to be—
Every eye there like a spoke in you centering,
You with your eloquence, blarney, and bantering—
All Vagabondia shouts at your entering,
King of the Tenderloin, Barney McGee!
There's no satiety
In your society
With the variety
Of your *esprit*.
Here's a long purse to you,
And a great thirst to you!
Fate be no worse to you,
Barney McGee!

Och, and the girls whose poor hearts you deracinate,
Whirl and bewilder and flutter and fascinate!
Faith, it's so killing you are, you assassinate—
Murder's the word for you, Barney McGee!
Bold when they're sunny, and smooth when they're
       showery—
Oh, but the style of you, fluent and flowery!
Chesterfield's way, with a touch of the Bowery!
How would they silence you, Barney machree?
Naught can your gab allay,
Learned as Rabelais
(You in his abbey lay

Once on the spree).
Here's to the smile of you,
(Oh, but the guile of you!)
And a long while of you,
Barney McGee!

Facile with phrases of length and Latinity,
Like honorificabilitudinity,
Where is the maid could resist your vicinity,
Wiled by the impudent grace of your plea?
Then your vivacity and pertinacity
Carry the day with the divil's audacity;
No more veracity robs your sagacity
Of perspicacity, Barney McGee.
When all is new to them,
What will you do to them?
Will you be true to them?
Who shall decree?
Here's a fair strife to you!
Health and long life to you!
And a great wife to you, Barney McGee!

Barney McGee, you're the pick of gentility;
Nothing can phase you, you've such a facility;
Nobody ever yet found your utility—
There is the charm of you, Barney McGee;
Under conditions that others would stammer in,
Still unperturbed as a cat or a Cameron,
Polished as somebody in the Decameron,
Putting the glamour on price or Pawnee.
In your meanderin',
Love and philanderin',
Calm as a mandarin

Sipping his tea!
Under the art of you,
Parcel and part of you,
Here's to the heart of you,
Barney McGee!

You who were ever alert to befriend a man,
You who were ever the first to defend a man,
You who had always the money to lend a man,
Down on his luck and hard up for a V!
Sure, you'll be playing a harp in beatitude
(And a quare sight you will be in that attitude)—
Some day, where gratitude seems but a platitude,
You'll find your latitude, Barney McGee.
That's no flim-flam at all,
Frivol or sham at all,
Just the plain—Damn it all,
Have one with me!
Here's one and more to you!
Friends by the score to you,
True to the core to you,
Barney McGee!

JULIA WARD HOWE
1819—1910

BATTLE HYMN OF THE REPUBLIC

MINE eyes have seen the glory of the coming of the
    Lord,
He is trampling out the vintage where the grapes of
    wrath are stored;
He hath loosed the fateful lightning of his terrible
    swift sword,
        His truth is marching on.

I have seen him in the watch-fires of a hundred cir-
    cling camps,
They have builded him an altar in the evening dews
    and damps;
I can read his righteous sentence by the dim and
    flaring lamps,
        His day is marching on.

I have read a fiery gospel writ in burnished rows of
    steel:
"As ye deal with my contemners, so with you my
    grace shall deal;
Let the hero, born of woman, crush the serpent with
    his heel,
        Since God is marching on."

He has sounded forth the trumpet that shall never
    call retreat,
He is sifting out the hearts of men before his judg-
    ment seat.
Oh, be swift, my soul, to answer him! be jubilant,
    my feet!
        Our God is marching on.

In the beauty of the lilies, Christ was born across the
    sea,
With a glory in his bosom that transfigures you and
    me;
As he died to make men holy, let us die to set men
    free,
        While God is marching on.

WILLIAM DEAN HOWELLS
1837—1920

HEREDITY

THAT swollen paunche you are doomed to bear
Your gluttonous grandsire used to wear:
That tongue, at once so light and dull,
Wagged in your grandam's empty skull;
That leering of the sensual eye
Your father, when he came to die,
Left yours alone: and that cheap flirt,
Your mother, gave you from the dirt
The simper which she used upon
So many men ere he was won.

Your vanity and greed and lust
Are each your portion from the dust
Of those that died, and from the tomb
Made you what you must needs become.
I do not hold you aught to blame
For sin at second hand, and shame:
Evil could but from evil spring;
And yet, away, you charnel thing!

VICTOR HUGO
France
1802—1885

TO A WOMAN

CHILD! if I were a king, my throne I would surrender,
   My scepter, and my car, and kneeling vavas-
sours,

My golden crown, and porphyry baths, and consorts
   tender,
And fleets that fill the seas, and regal pomp and
   splendor,
  All for one look of yours!

If I were God, the earth and luminous deeps that
   span it,
  Angels and demons bowed beneath my word
   divine,
Chaos profound, with flanks of flaming gold and
   granite,
Eternity, and space, and sky, and sun, and planet,
  All for one kiss of thine.

     Translated by W. J. Robertson

THE DJINNS

   Town, tower,
   Shore, deep,
   Where lower
   Cliffs steep;
   Where play
   Winds gay,—
   All sleep.

   Hark! a sound,
   Far and slight,
   Breathes around
   On the night:
   High and higher,
   Nigh and nigher,
   Like a fire
   Roaring bright.

Now on 'tis sweeping
With rattling beat,
Like dwarf imp leaping
In gallop fleet:
He flies, he prances,
In frolic fancies,
On wave-crest dances
With pattering feet.

Hark, the rising swell,
With each nearer burst!
Like the toll of bell
Of a convent cursed;
Like the billowy roar
On a storm-lashed shore,—
Now hushed, now once more
Maddening to its worst.

O God! the deadly sound
Of the Djinns' fearful cry!
Quick, 'neath the spiral round
Of the deep staircase fly!
See, see our lamplight fade!
And of the balustrade
Mounts, mounts the circling shade
Up to the ceiling high!

'Tis the Djinns' wild streaming swarm
Whistling in their tempest-flight;
Snap the tall yews 'neath the storm,
Like a pine-flame crackling bright.
Swift and heavy, lo, their crowd
Through the heavens rushing loud,

Like a livid thunder-cloud
With its bolt of fiery night!

Ha! they are on us, close without!
Shut tight the shelter where we lie!
With hideous din the monster rout,
Dragon and vampire, fill the sky!
The loosened rafter overhead
Trembles and bends like quivering reed;
Shakes the old door with shuddering dread,
As from its rusty hinge 'twould fly!

Wild cries of hell! voices that howl and shriek!
The horrid swarm before the tempest tossed—
O Heaven!—descends my lowly roof to seek:
Bends the strong wall beneath the furious host.
Totters the house, as though, like dry leaf shorn
From autumn bough and on the mad blast borne,
Up from its deep foundations it were torn
To join the stormy whirl. Ah! all is lost!

O Prophet! if thy hand but now
Save from these foul and hellish things,
A pilgrim at thy shrine I'll bow,
Laden with pious offerings.
Bid their hot breath its fiery rain
Stream on my faithful door in vain,
Vainly upon my blackened pane
Grate the fierce claws of their dark wings!

They have passed!—and their wild legion
Cease to thunder at my door;
Fleeting through night's rayless region,
Hither they return no more.

Clanking chains and sounds of woe
Fill the forests as they go;
And the tall oaks cower low,
Bent their flaming flight before.

On! on! the storm of wings
Bears far the fiery fear,
Till scarce the breeze now brings
Dim murmurings to the ear;
Like locusts' humming hail,
Or thrash of tiny flail
Plied by the pattering hail
On some old roof-tree near.

Fainter now are borne
Fitful mutterings still;
As, when Arab horn
Swells its magic peal,
Shoreward o'er the deep
Fairy voices sweep,
And the infant's sleep
Golden visions fill.

Each deadly Djinn,
Dark child of fright,
Of death and sin,
Speeds the wild flight.
Hark, the dull moan,
Like the deep tone
Of ocean's groan,
Afar, by night!

More and more
Fades it now,

VICTOR HUGO

As on shore
Ripple's flow,—
As the plaint
Far and faint
Of a saint
Murmured low.

Hark! hist!
Around,
I list!
The bounds
Of space
All trace
Efface
Of sound.

HER NAME

A LILY's fragrance rare, an aureole's pale splendor,
    The whisper of the waning day;
Love's passionate pure kiss of virginal surrender;
The hour that breathes farewell, mysterious and
            tender;
    The grief by comfort charmed away;

The sevenfold scarf by storm emblazed and braiden,
    A trophy to the victor sun;
The sudden cadence of a voice with memories laden;
The soft and simple vow from a shamefac'd maiden;
    The dream of a new life begun;

The murmur that with orient Dawn, rising to greet
        her,
    From lips of fabled Memnon came;

The undulant hum remote of some melodious
        meter:—
All the soul dreams most sweet, if aught than these
        be sweeter,
    O Lyre, is less sweet than her name!

Even as a muttered prayer pronounce it, breathing
        lowly,
    But let it sound through all our songs!
Be in the darkened shrine the one light dim and holy!
Be as the world divine that same voice, chaunting
        slowly
    From the deep altar-place prolongs!

O world! ere yet my Muse, upborne in ample azure,
    Her wings for wandering flight unfolds,
And with those clamorous names, profaned of pride
        or pleasure,
Dares blend that chaster one that, like a sacred
        treasure,
    Love hidden in my heart still holds,

Needs must my song, while yet of silence unfor-
        saken,
    Be like those hymns we kneel to hear,
And with its solemn strains the tremulous air awaken,
As though, with viewless plumes and unseen censers
        shaken,
    A flight of angels hovered near!

LEIGH HUNT
1784—1859
ABOU BEN ADHEM

ABOU BEN ADHEM (may his tribe increase!)
Awoke one night from a deep dream of peace,
And saw, within the moonlight in his room,
Making it rich, and like a lily in bloom,
An Angel writing in a book of gold:
Axceeding peace had made Ben Adhem bold,
And to the Presence in the room he said,
"What writest thou?" The Vision raised its head,

And with a look made of all sweet accord
Answered, "The names of those who love the Lord."
"And is mine one?" said Abou. "Nay, not so,"
Replied the Angel. Abou spoke more low,
But cheerly still, and said, "I pray thee, then,
Write me as one that loves his fellow-men."

The Angel wrote, and vanished. The next night
It came again with a great wakening light,
And showed the names whom love of God had
        blessed;
And lo! Ben Adhem's name led all the rest!

JENNY KISSED ME

JENNY kissed me when we met,
    Jumping from the chair she sat in.
Time, you thief! who love to get
    Sweets into your list, put that in.

Say I'm weary, say I'm sad;
Say that health and wealth have missed me;
Say I'm growing old, but add—
                    Jenny kissed me!

JAFFAR

JAFFAR, the Barmecide, the good vizier,
The poor man's hope, the friend without a peer—
Jaffar was dead, slain by a doom unjust;
And guilty Haroun, sullen with mistrust
Of what the good, and even the bad, might say,
Ordained that no man living, from that day,
Should dare to speak his name on pain of death.
All Araby and Persia held their breath;
All but the brave Mondeer: he, proud to show
How far for love a grateful soul could go,
And facing death for very scorn and grief
(For his great heart wanted a great relief)
Stood forth in Bagdad, daily, in the square
Where once had stood a happy house, and there
Harangued the tremblers at the scimitar
On all they owed to the divine Jaffar.

"Bring me this man," the caliph cried; the man
Was brought, was gazed upon. The mutes began
To bind his arms. "Welcome, brave cords," cried he,
"From bonds far worse Jaffar delivered me;
From wants, from shames, from loveless household
                    fears;
Made a man's eyes friends with delicious tears;
Restored me, loved me, put me on a par
With his great self. How can I pay Jaffar?"

HENDRIK IBSEN

Haroun, who felt that on a soul like this
The mightiest vengeance could but fall amiss,
Now deigned to smile, as one great lord of fate
Might smile upon another half as great.
He said, "Let worth grow frenzied if it will;
The caliph's judgment shall be master still.
Go, and since gifts so move thee, take this gem,
The richest in the Tartar's diadem,
And hold the giver as thou deemest fit!"
"Gifts!" cried the friend; he took and holding it,
High toward the heavens, as though to meet his
      star,
Exclaimed, "This, too, I owe to thee, Jaffar!"

HENDRIK IBSEN
1828—1906
NORWEGIAN

A SWAN

My white and glistening
    Swan, my mute one—
    Who wouldst not flute one
Note for my listening—

Fearfully hiding
    Thy song's hushed spirit,
Didst thou pass gliding,
    Nor let'st me hear it.

But, ere we parted,
    Once, eyes replied to me,
    Lips vowed and lied to me,
And song upstarted:

'Twas one brief quiring
And thy day gone then.
Thou sang'st expiring—
Thou wast a swan, then!

Translated by F. E. Garrett

SOLVEIG'S SONG

MAYBE both the snowtime and the springtime will go,
And summer after that, and the whole year so;
But some day thou art coming, full sure I know,
And I shall be waiting, for I promised thee so.

God strengthen thee faring by sea or land—
God gladden thee if at His footstool thou stand.
While thou art coming I shall wait for thee here;
And waitest thou in heaven, I'll meet thee there,
        my Dear.

Translated by F. E. Garrett

THE PETREL

THE storm-petrel broods where soundings fail;—
'Twas an old sea-captain told me the tale.

Of surf and spindrift her plumage drinks;
She treads the rollers and never sinks.

With the sea she will fall; with the sea will rise;
In calm she is mute; at the tempest she cries.

Something 'twixt flying and swimming it is,
A dream between heaven and hell's abyss.

JOHN JAMES INGALLS

Too light for the waves, too heavy for air—:
Ah! bird and bard,—our trouble is there!

And the worst of it is, to the ears of the wise,
Most of the story is old salt's lies.

Translated by F. E. Garrett

JOHN JAMES INGALLS
1833—1900

OPPORTUNITY

MASTER of human destinies am I.
Fame, love, and fortune on my footsteps wait,
Cities and fields I walk; I penetrate
Deserts and seas remote, and, passing by
Hovel, and mart, and palace, soon or late
I knock unbidden, once at every gate!
If sleeping, wake—if feasting, rise before
I turn away. It is the hour of fate,
And they who follow me reach every state
Mortals desire, and conquer every foe
Save death; but those who doubt or hesitate,
Condemned to failure, penury and woe,
Seek me in vain and uselessly implore—
I answer not, and I return no more.

JEAN INGELOW
1820—1897

THE HIGH TIDE ON THE COAST OF LINCOLNSHIRE

THE old mayor climb'd the belfry tower,
  The ringers ran by two, by three;
"Pull, if ye never pull'd before;
  Good ringers, pull your best," quoth he.
"Play uppe, play uppe, O Boston bells!
Ply all your changes, all your swells,
  Play uppe, 'The Brides of Enderby.'"

Men say it was a stolen tyde—
  The Lord that sent it, He knows all;
But in myne ears doth still abide
  The message that the bells let fall:
And there was nought of strange, beside
The flight of mews and peewits pied
  By millions crouch'd on the old sea wall.

I sat and spun within the doore,
  My thread brake off, I rais'd myne eyes;
The level sun, like ruddy ore,
  Lay sinking in the barren skies;
And dark against day's golden death
She moved where Lindis wandereth,
My sonne's faire wife, Elizabeth.

"Cusha! Cusha! Cusha!" calling,
Ere the early dews were falling,
Farre away I heard her song,
"Cusha! Cusha!" all along;

JEAN INGELOW

Where the reedy Lindis floweth,
   Floweth, floweth,
From the meads where melick groweth
Faintly came her milking song—

"Cusha! Cusha! Cusha!" calling,
"For the dews will soone be falling;
Leave your meadow grasses mellow,
   Mellow, mellow;
Quit your cowslips, cowslips yellow;
Come uppe, Whitefoot, come uppe, Lightfoot;
Quit the stalks of parsley hollow,
   Hollow, hollow;
Come uppe, Jetty, rise and follow,
From the clovers lift your head;
Come uppe, Whitefoot, come uppe, Lightfoot,
Come uppe, Jetty, rise and follow,
Jetty, to the milking shed."

If it be long, ay, long ago,
   When I beginne to think howe long,
Againe I hear the Lindis flow,
   Swift as an arrowe, sharpe and strong;
And all the aire, it seemeth mee,
Bin full of floating bells (sayth shee),
That ring the tune of Enderby.

Alle fresh the level pasture lay,
   And not a shadowe mote be seene,
Save where full fyve good miles away
   The steeple tower'd from out the greene;
And lo! the great bell farre and wide
Was heard in all the country side
That Saturday at eventide.

The swanherds where their sedges are
   Mov'd on in sunset's golden breath,
The shepherde lads I heard afarre,
   And my sonne's wife, Elizabeth;
Till floating o'er the grassy sea
Came downe that kyndly message free,
The "Brides of Mavis Enderby."

Then some look'd uppe into the sky,
   And all along where Lindis flows
To where the goodly vessels lie,
   And where the lordly steeple shows.
They sayde, "And why should this thing be?
What danger lowers by land or sea?
They ring the tune of Enderby!

"For evil news from Mablethorpe,
   Of pyrate galleys warping down;
For shippes ashore beyond the scorpe,
   They have not spar'd to wake the towne:
But while the west bin red to see,
And storms be none, and pyrates flee,
Why ring 'The Brides of Enderby' ? "

I look'd without, and lo! my sonne
   Came riding downe with might and main:
He rais'd a shout as he drew on,
   Till all the welkin rang again,
"Elizabeth! Elizabeth!"
(A sweeter woman ne'er drew breath
Than my sonne's wife, Elizabeth.)

"The olde sea wall (he cried) is downe,
   The rising tide comes on apace,

And boats adrift in yonder towne
   Go sailing uppe the market-place."
He shook as one that looks on death:
"God save you, mother!" straight he saith;
"Where is my wife, Elizabeth?"

"Good sonne, where Lindis winds her way,
   With her two bairns I marked her long;
And ere yon bells beganne to play
   Afar I heard her milking song."
He looked across the grassy lea,
To right, to left, "Ho, Enderby!"
They rang "The Brides of Enderby!"

With that he cried and beat his breast;
   For, lo! along the river's bed
A mighty eygre rear'd his crest,
   And uppe the Lindis raging sped.
It swept with thunderous noises loud;
Shap'd like a curling snow-white cloud,
Or like a demon in a shroud.

And rearing Lindis backward press'd
   Shook all her trembling bankes amaine;
Then madly at the eygre's breast
   Flung uppe her weltering walls again.
Then bankes came downe with ruin and rout—
Then beaten foam flew round about—
Then all the mighty floods were out.

So farre, so fast the eygre drave,
   The heart had hardly time to beat
Before a shallow seething wave
   Sobb'd in the grasses at oure feet:

The feet had hardly time to flee
Before it brake against the knee,
And all the world was in the sea.

Upon the roofe we sate that night,
  The noise of bells went sweeping by;
I mark'd the lofty beacon light
  Stream from the church tower, red and high—
A lurid mark and dread to see;
And awsome bells they were to mee,
That in the dark rang "Enderby."

They rang the sailor lads to guide
  From roofe to roofe who fearless row'd;
And I—my sonne was at my side,
  And yet the ruddy beacon glow'd:
And yet he moan'd beneath his breath,
"O come in life, or come in death!
O lost! my love, Elizabeth."

And didst thou visit him no more?
  Thou didst, thou didst, my daughter deare;
The waters laid thee at his doore,
  Ere yet the early dawn was clear.
Thy pretty bairns in fast embrace,
The lifted sun shone on thy face,
Downe drifted to thy dwelling-place.

That flow strew'd wrecks about the grass,
  That ebbe swept out the flocks to sea:
A fatal ebbe and flow, alas!
  To many more than myne and mee;
But each will mourn his own (she saith);
And sweeter woman ne'er drew breath
Than my sonne's wife, Elizabeth.

I shall never hear her more
  By the reedy Lindis shore,
"Cusha! Cusha! Cusha!" calling,
  Ere the early dews be falling;
I shall never hear her song,
"Cusha! Cusha!" all along
Where the sunny Lindis floweth,
  Goeth, floweth;
From the meads where melick groweth,
  When the water winding down,
  Onward floweth to the town.

I shall never see her more
Where the reeds and rushes quiver,
  Shiver, quiver;
Stand beside the sobbing river,
Sobbing, throbbing, in its falling
To the sandy lonesome shore;
I shall never hear her calling,
"Leave your meadow grasses mellow,
  Mellow, mellow;
Quit your cowslips, cowslips yellow;
Come uppe, Whitefoot, come uppe, Lightfoot;
Quit your pipes of parsley hollow,
  Hollow, hollow;
Come uppe, Lightfoot, rise and follow;
  Lightfoot, Whitefoot,
From your clovers lift the head;
Come uppe, Jetty, follow, follow,
Jetty, to the milking shed."

ROBERT G. INGERSOLL
1833—1899
LIFE IS A NARROW VALE

LIFE is a narrow vale between the cold
And barren peaks of two eternities.
We strive in vain to look beyond the heights,
We cry aloud; the only answer
Is the echo of our wailing cry.
From the voiceless lips of the unreplying dead
There comes no word; but in the night of death
Hope sees a star, and listening love can hear
The rustle of a wing.
These myths were born of hopes, and fears and tears,
And smiles; and they were touched and colored
By all there is of joy and grief between
The rosy dawn of birth and death's sad night;
They clothed even the stars with passion,
And gave to gods the faults and frailties
Of the sons of men. In them the winds
And waves were music, and all the lakes and streams,
Springs, mountains, woods, and perfumed dells,
Were haunted by a thousand fairy forms.

WALLACE IRWIN
1876—
FROM ROMANY TO ROME

UPON the road to Romany
  It's stay, friend, stay!
There's lots o' love and lots o' time
  To linger on the way;

Poppies for the twilight,
  Roses for the noon,
It's happy goes as lucky goes
  To Romany in June.

But on the road to Rome—oh
  It's march, man, march!
The dust is on the chariot wheels,
  The sere is on the larch;
Helmets and javelins
  And bridles flecked with foam,—
The flowers are dead, the world's ahead
  Upon the road to Rome.

But on the road to Rome—ah,
  It's fight, man, fight!
Footman and horseman
  Treading left and right,
Camp-fires and watch-fires
  Ruddying the gloam—
The fields are gray and worn away
  Along the road to Rome.

Upon the road to Romany
  It's sing, boys, sing!
Though rag and pack be on our back
  We'll whistle at the King.
Wine is in the sunshine
  Madness in the moon,
And de'il may care the road we fare
  To Romany in June.

Along the road to Rome, alas!
　　The glorious dust is whirled,
Strong hearts are fierce to see
　　The City of the World;
Yet footfall or bugle-call
　　Or thunder as ye will,
Upon the road to Romany
　　The birds are calling still!

SONG FOR A CRACKED VOICE

WHEN I was young and slender, a spender, a lender,
　　What gentleman adventurer was prankier than I,
Who lustier at passes with glasses—and lasses,
　　How pleasant was the look of 'em as I came
　　　jaunting by!
　　(But now there's none to sigh at me as I come
　　　creaking by.)

Then Pegasus went loping 'twixt hoping and toping,
　　A song in every dicky-bird, a scent in every rose;
What moons for lovelorn glances, romances, and
　　dances,
　　And how the spirit of the waltz went thrilling
　　　to my toes!
　　(Egad, it's now a gouty pang goes thrilling to
　　　my toes!)

Was I that lover frantic, romantic, and antic,
　　Who found the lute in Molly's voice, the heaven
　　　in her eyes?
Who, madder than a hatter, talked patter? No matter.

Call not that little, youthful ghost, but leave it
    where it lies!
(Dear, dear how many winter snows have drifted
    where she lies!)

But now I'm old and humble, why mumble and
    grumble
    At all the posy-linked rout that hurries laughing
    by?
Framed in my gold-rimmed glasses each lass is who
    passes
    And Youth is still a-twinkling in the corner of
    my eye.
(How strange you cannot see it in the corner of
    my eye!)

WILL IRWIN
1873—

HEROIC BALLAD, 1976

*The Battle Song of Flight-Lieutenant Ehrlich Fara-
day Miller, Aerial Gas Corps.*

ALL hail the sturdy vats and tanks
    That brewed the gas of victory,
And hail, all hail thy patriot ranks—
    Industrial Chemistry!

And hail Field Marshal Poggleburg,
    That miracle of chemic lore,
Who gave our land its bulwark firm—
    $Z^7 CO^4$!

The tocsin tapped at 8.15;
 At 9 we slipped our mooring-mast,
And ere 11.55
 Our far frontier was passed.

My vision plumbed the midnight deeps
 And saw our mobile retorts glow,
A line of light from sky to sky
 Eight thousand yards below.

Ah, swift our strutted vulture sped
 Its plotted course; but swifter still
The lethal gas that laughs at masks
 Enshrouded vale and hill.

Ye footmen of our Chemic Corps,
 How well ye plied your task that night!
Three thousand thousand hostile eyes
 Saw not the morrow's light.

But nobler patriot aim was ours
 That down the midnight air-lane flew—
Ye hawks of vengeance, steel your souls!
 Your reckoning be true!

We sought his city's wide expanse
 Whence all his railroad lines were laid,
And where ten million perjured hands
 Maintained his export trade.

My dial swung to eight-point-four;
 The speaking-signal gleamed—and lo,
Our chieftain's accents rang along
 The tunéd radio!

WILL IRWIN

"Men, yonder sleeps the invidious brood
  Whose greed has raised our ocean freights
And put upon our pork and prunes
  Discriminating rates.

"Wise bombsmen, draw your cosines true!
  Wild wingmen, speed as ne'er before
Your answer to their bootless taunts—
  Z^7 CO^4!"

With His eternal aniline
  The Almighty Chemist hued the skies;
Ah, spread ye fair, my gallant gas—
  To-day the foeman dies!

And now the imperial city stretched
  Its checkered roofs across the plain—
I threw my firing-lever home
  And loosed our chemic rain.

A moment all my senses reeled,
  A moment scare I dared to hope;
Then cleared mine anxious eyes! I seized
  My teleperiscope.

I focused on a city street
  A film of mist and naught beside—
Till from the doors contorted throngs
  Burst quivering—and died.

O'er dome and stack my lens I swept,
  O'er park and stately avenue—
Ah, stout Z^7 CO^4.
  How swift thy stroke, how true!

And did I pity, comrades? Ay,
  As he who slaughters for our feast
May drop one unrestraining tear
  Above the shambled beast.

These were not Nordics; let them die!
  A lesser folk, decadent, frail;
Scarce reached they six-point-forty on
  The anthropometric scale!

From roofs and spires the untended fires
  Smoked sullen to our rudder-gears;
The squadrons wheeled; the wave-lengths
    reeled
  With gay, exultant cheers.

Home, heroes, to your ransomed land;
  See yonder how her steel-works gleam!
Ho, Eagles! From her pylons tall
  Victorious banners stream!

Enraptured kisses wait your lips
  And bosoms warm invite your rest
Of Nordic maids with Class A minds
  Upon the Binet test.

And ere the fiscal year was done
  Our trade had won its guerdon due;
Our balance rose from three per cent.
  To four-point-forty-two.

SAMUEL JOHNSON
1709—1784
ONE-AND-TWENTY

LONG-EXPECTED One-and-Twenty,
  Lingering year at length is flown:
Pride and pleasure, pomp and plenty,
  Great Sir John, are now your own.

Loosened from the minor's tether,
  Free to mortgage or to sell,
Wild as wind and light as feather,
  Bid the sons of thrift farewell.

Call the Betsies, Kates and Jennies,
  All the names that banish care;
Lavish of your grandsire's guineas,
  Show the spirit of an heir.

All that prey on vice and folly
  Joy to see their quarry fly:
There's the gamester, light and jolly,
  There's the lender, grave and sly.

Wealth, my lad, was made to wander,
  Let it wander as it will;
Call the jockey, call the pander,
  Bid them come and take their fill.

When the bonny blade carouse.,
  Pockets full and spirits high—
What are acres? what are houses?
  Only dirt, or wet or dry.

Should the guardian friend or mother
   Tell the woes of wilful waste,
Scorn their counsel, scorn their pother;
   You can hang or drown at last!

SIR WILLIAM JONES
1746—1794

WHAT CONSTITUTES A STATE?

WHAT constitutes a State?
   Not high-raised battlement or labored mound,
   Thick wall or moated gate—
Not cities proud with spires and turrets crowned—
   Not bays and broad-armed ports,
Where, laughing at the storm, rich navies ride—
   Not starred and spangled courts,
Where low-browed baseness wafts perfume to pride.
   No; men, high-minded men,
With powers as far above dull brutes endued
   In forest, brake or den,
As beasts excel cold rocks and brambles rude;
   Men who their duties know,
But know their rights, and, knowing, dare maintain,
   Prevent the long-aimed blow,
And crush the tyrant while they rend the chain—
   These constitute a State:
And sovereign Law, that State's collected will,
   O'er thrones and globes elate
Sits empress, crowning good, repressing ill.
   Smit by her sacred frown,
The fiend, Dissension, like a vapor sinks;
   And even the all-dazzling crown

Hides his faint rays, and at her bidding shrinks.
  Such was this heaven loved isle,
Than Lesbos fairer, and the Cretan shore!
  No more shall freedom smile?
Shall Britons languish, and be men no more?
  Since all must life resign,
Those sweet rewards which decorate the brave
  'Tis folly to decline,
And steal inglorious to the silent grave.

BEN JOHNSON
1573—1637

HEAR ME, O GOD

Hear me, O God!
    A broken heart
    Is my best part:
Use still Thy rod,
    That I may prove
    Therein Thy love.

If Thou hadst not
    Been stern to me,
    But left me free,
I had forgot
    Myself and Thee.

For sin's so sweet,
    As minds ill bent
    Rarely repent,
Until they meet
    Their punishment.

HYMN TO DIANA

Queen and Huntress, chaste and fair,
  Now the sun is laid to sleep,
Seated in thy silver chair,
    State in wonted manner keep:
      Hesperus entreats thy light,
      Goddess excellently bright.

Earth, let not thy envious shade
  Dare itself to interpose;
Cynthia's shining orb was made
    Heaven to clear when day did close:
      Bless us then with wishèd sight,
      Goddess excellently bright.

Lay thy bow of pearl apart
  And thy crystal-shining quiver;
Give unto the flying hart
    Space to breathe, how short soever:
      Thou that mak'st a day of night,
      Goddess excellently bright!

THE NOBLE NATURE

It is not growing like a tree
  In bulk, doth make Man better be;
Or standing long an oak, three hundred year,
To fall a log at last, dry, bald, and sere:
      A lily of a day
      Is fairer far in May,
    Although it fall and die that night—
    It was the plant and flower of Light.
In small proportions we just beauties see;
And in short measures life may perfect be.

TO CELIA

Drink to me only with thine eyes,
    And I will pledge with mine;
Or leave a kiss but in the cup
    And I'll not look for wine.
The thirst that from the soul doth rise
    Doth ask a drink divine;
But might I of Jove's nectar sup,
      I would not change for thine.

I sent thee late a rosy wreath,
    Not so much honoring thee
As giving it a hope that there
    It could not wither'd be;
But thou thereon didst only breathe
    And sent'st it back to me;
Since when it grows, and smells, I swear,
    Not of itself but thee!

JACK JUDGE AND HARRY WILLIAMS
"IT'S A LONG, LONG WAY TO TIPPERARY"

Up to mighty London came an Irishman one day,
As the streets are paved with gold, sure ev'ry-one
    was gay;
Singing songs of Piccadilly,
Strand and Leicester Square,
Till Paddy got excited, then he shouted to them
    there:—

Chorus

"It's a long way to Tipperary,
It's a long way to go: It's a long way to Tipperary,
To the sweetest girl I know!

Good-bye Piccadilly,
Fare-well, Leicester Square,
It's a long, long way to Tipperary,
But my heart's right there!"

Paddy wrote a letter to his Irish Molly O',
Saying, "Should you not receive it, write and let me
    know!
If I make mistakes in 'spelling,'
"Molly dear," said he,
"Remember it's the pen that's bad, don't lay the
    blame on me."

Molly wrote a neat reply to Irish Paddy O',
Saying, "Mike Maloney wants to marry me, and so
Leave the Strand and Piccadilly, or you'll be to
    blame,
For love has fairly drove me silly—hoping you're
    the same!"

KAO SHIH

CHINESE

DESOLATION

THERE was a King of Liang—a king of wondrous
    might—
Who kept an open palace, where music charmed the
    night—

Since he was Lord of Liang a thousand years have
    flown,
And of the towers he builded yon ruins stands alone.

There reigns a heavy silence; gaunt weeds through
    windows pry,
And down the streets of Liang old echoes, wailing,
    die.

JOHN KEATS
1795—1821

A THING OF BEAUTY

A THING of beauty is a joy for ever:
Its loveliness increases; it will never
Pass into nothingness; but still will keep
A bower quiet for us, and a sleep
Full of sweet dreams, and health, and quiet breathing.
Therefore, on every morrow, are we wreathing
A flowery band to bind us to the earth,
Spite of despondence, of the inhuman dearth
Of noble natures, of the gloomy days,
Of all the unhealthy and o'er-darkened ways
Made for our searching: yes, in spite of all,
Some shape of beauty moves away the pall
From our dark spirits. Such the sun, the moon,
Trees old and young, sprouting a shady boon
For simple sheep; and such are daffodils,
With the green world they live in; and clear rills
That for themselves a cooling covert make
'Gainst the hot season; the mid-forest brake,
Rich with a sprinkling of fair musk-rose blooms;
And such too is the grandeur of the dooms
We have imagined for the mighty dead;
All lovely tales that we have heard or read:
An endless fountain of immortal drink,
Pouring unto us from the Heaven's brink,

Nor do we merely feel these essences
For one short hour; no, even as the trees
That whisper round, a Temple becomes soon
Dear as the Temple's self, so does the moon,
The passion poesy, glories infinite,
Haunt us till they become a cheering light
Unto our souls, and bound to us so fast,
That, whether there be shine or gloom o'ercast,
They always must be with us, or we die.

ODE TO A NIGHTINGALE

My heart aches, and a drowsy numbness pains
   My sense, as though of hemlock I had drunk,
Or emptied some dull opiate to the drains
   One minute past, and Lethe-wards had sunk:
'Tis not through envy of thy happy lot,
   But being too happy in thy happiness,
      That thou, light-wingèd Dryad of the trees,
      In some melodious plot
Of beechen green and shadows numberless,
   Singest of summer in full-throated ease.

O for a draught of vintage! that hath been
   Cooled a long age in the deep-delvèd earth,
Tasting of Flora and the country-green,
   Dance, and Provençal song, and sunburnt mirth!
O for a beaker full of the warm South!
   Full of the true, the blushful Hippocrene,
      With beaded bubbles winking at the brim,
      And purple-stainèd mouth;
That I might drink, and leave the world unseen,
   And with thee fade away into the forest dim:

JOHN KEATS

Fade far away, dissolve, and quite forget
   What thou among the leaves hast never known,
The weariness, the fever, and the fret
   Here, where men sit and hear each other groan;
Where palsy shakes a few, sad, last grey hairs,
   Where youth grows pale, and spectre-thin, and
          dies;
      Where but to think is to be full of sorrow
        And leaden-eyed despairs;
Where beauty cannot keep her lustrous eyes,
   Or new Love pine at them beyond to-morrow.

Away! away! for I will fly to thee,
   Not charioted by Bacchus and his pards,
But on the viewless wings of Poesy,
   Though the dull brain perplexes and retards:
Already with thee! tender is the night,
   And haply the Queen-Moon is on her throne,
     Clustered around by all her starry Fays;
       But here there is no light,
Save what from heaven is with the breezes blown
   Through verdurous glooms and winding mossy
     ways.

I cannot see what flowers are at my feet,
   Nor what soft incense hangs upon the boughs,
But, in embalmèd darkness, guess each sweet
   Wherewith the seasonable month endows
The grass, the thicket, and the fruit-tree wild;
   White hawthorn, and the pastoral eglantine;
     Fast-fading violets covered up in leaves;
       And mid-May's eldest child,
The coming musk-rose, full of dewy wine,
   The murmurous haunt of flies on summer eyes.

Darkling I listen; and for many a time
  I have been half in love with easeful Death,
Called him soft names in many a musèd rhyme,
  To take into the air my quiet breath;
Now more than ever seems it rich to die,
  To cease upon the midnight with no pain,
    While thou art pouring forth thy soul abroad
      In such an ecstasy!
    Still would'st thou sing, and I have ears in
      vain—
    To thy high requiem become a sod.

Thou wast not born for death, immortal Bird!
  No hungry generations tread thee down;
The voice I hear this passing night was heard
  In ancient days by emperor and clown:
Perhaps the self-same song that found a path
  Through the sad heart of Ruth, when, sick for
    home,
    She stood in tears amid the alien corn;
      The same that oft-times hath
  Charmed magic casements, opening on the foam
    Of perilous seas, in faery lands forlorn.

Forlorn! the very word is like a bell
  To toll me back from thee to my sole self!
Adieu! the fancy cannot cheat so well
  As she is famed to do, deceiving elf.
Adieu! adieu! thy plaintive anthem fades
  Past the near meadows, over the still stream,
    Up the hill-side; and now 'tis buried deep
      In the next valley-glades:
  Was it a vision, or a waking dream?
    Fled is that music—do I wake or sleep?

JOHN KEATS

ODE ON A GRECIAN URN

THOU still unravished bride of quietness,
　　Thou foster-child of Silence and slow Time,
Sylvan historian, who canst thus express
　　A flowery tale more sweetly than our rhyme:
What leaf-fringed legend haunts about thy shape
　　Of deities or mortals, or of both,
　　　　In Tempe or the dales of Arcady?
　　What men or gods are these? What maidens loth?
What mad pursuit? What struggle to escape?
　　　　What pipes and timbrels? What wild ecstasy?

Heard melodies are sweet, but those unheard
　　Are sweeter; therefore, ye soft pipes, play on;
Not to the sensual ear, but, more endeared,
　　Pipe to the spirit ditties of no tone:
Fair youth, beneath the trees, thou canst not leave
　　Thy song, nor ever can those trees be bare;
　　　　Bold Lover, never, never canst thou kiss,
Though winning near the goal—yet, do not grieve;
　　She cannot fade, though thou has not thy bliss,
　　For ever wilt thou love, and she be fair!

Ah, happy, happy boughs! that cannot shed
　　Your leaves, nor ever bid the Spring adieu;
And, happy melodist, unwearièd,
　　For ever piping songs for ever new;
More happy love! more happy, happy love!
　　For ever warm and still to be enjoyed,
　　　　For ever panting and for ever young;
All breathing human passion far above,
　　That leaves a heart high-sorrowful and cloyed,
　　　　A burning forehead, and a parching tongue.

Who are these coming to the sacrifice?
   To what green altar, O mysterious priest
Lead'st thou that heifer lowing at the skies,
    And all her silken flanks with garlands drest
What little town by river or sea-shore,
   Or mountain-built with peaceful citadel,
    Is emptied of its folk, this pious morn?
And, little town, thy streets for evermore
   Will silent be; and not a soul, to tell
    Why thou art desolate, can e'er return,

O attic shape! fair attitude! with brede
   Of marble men and maidens overwrought,
With forest branches and the trodden weed;
   Thou, silent form! dost tease us out of thought
As doth eternity. Cold Pastoral!
   When old age shall this generation waste,
    Thou shalt remain, in midst of other woe
Than ours, a friend to man, to whom thou say'st,
"Beauty is truth, truth beauty—that is all
   Ye know on earth, and all ye need to know."

BARDS OF PASSION AND OF MIRTH

Bards of Passion and of Mirth,
Ye have left your souls on earth!
Have ye souls in heaven too,
Double-lived in regions new?
Yes, and those of heaven commune
With the spheres of sun and moon;
With the noise of fountains wondrous,
And the parle of voices thunderous;
With the whisper of heaven's trees

And one another, in soft ease
Seated on Elysian lawns
Browsed by none but Dian's fawns;
Underneath large blue-bells tented,
Where the daisies are rose-scented,
And the rose herself has got
Perfume which on earth is not;
Where the nightingale doth sing
Not a senseless, trancèd thing,
But divine melodious truth;
Philosophic numbers smooth;
Tales and golden histories
Of heaven and its mysteries.

Thus ye live on high, and then
On the earth ye live again;
And the souls ye left behind you
Teach us, here, the way to find you,
Where your other souls are joying,
Never slumbered, never cloying.
Here, your earth-born souls still speak
To mortals, of their little week;
Of their sorrows and delights;
Of their passions and their spites;
Of their glory and their shame;
What doth strengthen and what maim.
Thus ye teach us, every day,
Wisdom, though fled far away.

Bards of Passion and of Mirth,
Ye have left your souls on earth!
Ye have souls in heaven too,
Double-lived in regions new!

SLEEP

From "Endymion"

O MAGIC sleep! O comfortable bird,
That broodest o'er the troubled sea of the mind
Till it is hushed and smooth! O unconfined
Restraint! imprisoned liberty! great key
To golden palaces, strange minstrelsy,
Fountains grotesque, new trees, bespangled caves,
Echoing grottoes, full of tumbling waves
And moonlight; ay, to all the mazy world
Of silvery enchantment!—who, upfurled
Beneath thy drowsy wing a triple hour,
But renovates and lives?

A HYMN TO PAN

From "Endymion"

"O THOU whose mighty palace roof doth hang
From jaggèd trunks, and overshadoweth
Eternal whispers, glooms, the birth, life, death
Of unseen flowers in heavy peacefulness;
Who lov'st to see the hamadryads dress
Their ruffled locks where meeting hazels darken;
And through whole solemn hours dost sit, and
    hearken
The dreary melody of bedded reeds—
In desolate places, where dank moisture breeds
The pipy hemlock to strange overgrowth;
Bethinking thee, how melancholy loth
Thou wast to lose fair Syrinx—do thou now,
By the love's milky brow!

By all the trembling mazes that she ran,
Hear us, great Pan!

"O thou for whose soul-soothing quiet, turtles
Passion their voices cooingly 'mong myrtles,
What time thou wanderest at eventide
Through the sunny meadows, that outskirt the side
Of thine enmossèd realms: O thou to whom
Broad-leaved fig-trees even now foredoom
Their ripened fruitage; yellow-girted bees
Their golden honeycombs; our village leas
Their fairest blossomed beans and poppied corn;
The chuckling linnet its five young unborn,
To sing for thee; low-creeping strawberries
Their summer coolness; pent-up butterflies
Their freckled wings; yea, the fresh-building year
All its completions—be quickly near,
By every wind that nods the mountain-pine,
O forester divine!

"Thou to whom every fawn and satyr flies
For willing service; whether to surprise
The squatted hare while in half-sleeping fit;
Or upward ragged precipices flit
To save poor lambkins from the eagle's maw;
Or by mysterious enticement draw
Bewildered shepherds to their path again;
Or to tread breathless round the frothy main,
And gather up all fancifullest shells
For thee to tumble into Naiads' cells,
And, being hidden, laugh at their out-peeping;
Or to delight thee with fantastic leaping,

The while they pelt each other on the crown
With silvery oak-apples, and fir-cones brown,—
By all the echoes that about thee ring,
Hear us, O satyr king!

ON FIRST LOOKING INTO CHAPMAN'S HOMER

MUCH have I travelled in the realms of gold,
   And many goodly states and kingdoms seen;
   Round many western islands have I been
Which bards in fealty to Apollo hold.
Oft of one wide expanse had I been told
   That deep-browed Homer ruled as his demesne:
   Yet did I never breathe its pure serene
Till I heard Chapman speak out loud and bold:

Then felt I like some watcher of the skies
   When a new planet swims into his ken;
Or like stout Cortez, when with eagle eyes
   He stared at the Pacific—and all his men
Looked at each other with a wild surmise—
   Silent, upon a peak in Darien.

THE MERMAID TAVERN

SOULS of Poets dead and gone,
What Elysium have ye known,
Happy field or mossy cavern,
Choicer than the Mermaid Tavern?
Have ye tippled drink more fine
Than mine host's Canary wine?
Or are fruits of Paradise
Sweeter than those dainty pies

Of venison? O generous food!
Dressed as though bold Robin Hood
Would, with his maid Marian,
Sup and bowse from horn and can.

I have heard that on a day
Mine host's sign-board flew away,
Nobody knew whither, till
An astrologer's old quill
To a sheepskin gave the story,
Said he saw you in your glory,
Underneath a new old sign
Sipping beverage divine,
And pledging with contented smack
The Mermaid in the Zodiac.

Souls of Poets dead and gone,
What Elysium have ye known,
Happy field or mossy cavern,
Choicer than the Mermaid Tavern?

LA BELLE DAME SANS MERCI

Ah, what can ail thee, knight-at-arms,
Alone and palely loitering?
The sedge is withered from the lake,
And no birds sing.

Ah, what can ail thee, knight-at-arms,
So haggard and so woe-begone?
The squirrel's granary is full,
And the harvest's done.

I see a lily on thy brow
With anguish moist and fever dew;

And on thy cheek a fading rose
    Fast withereth too.

I met a lady in the meads,
    Full beautiful—a faery's child,
Her hair was long, her foot was light,
    And her eyes were wild.

I made a garland for her head,
    And bracelets too, and fragrant zone;
She looked at me as she did love,
    And made sweet moan.

I set her on my pacing steed
    And nothing else saw all day long,
For sideways would she lean, and sing
    A faery's song.

She found me roots of relish sweet,
    And honey wild and manna-dew,
And sure in language strange she said,
    "I love thee true!"

She took me to her elfin grot,
    And there she wept and sighed full sore;
And there I shut her wild, wild eyes
    With kisses four.

And there she lullèd me asleep,
    And there I dreamed—Ah! woe betide!
The latest dream I ever dreamed
    On the cold hill's side.

I saw pale kings and princes too,
  Pale warriors, death-pale were they all;
Who cried—"La belle Dames sans merci
    Hath thee in thrall!"

I saw their starved lips in the gloom
  With horrid warning gapèd wide,
And I awoke and found me here
    On the cold hill's side.

And this is why I sojourn here
  Alone and palely loitering,
Though the sedge is withered from the lake,
    And no birds sing.

ODE TO AUTUMN

Season of mists and mellow fruitfulness!
  Close bosom-friend of the maturing sun;
Conspiring with him how to load and bless
  With fruit the vines that round the thatch-eaves
      run;
To bend with apples the mossed cottage-trees,
  And fill all fruit with ripeness to the core;
    To swell the gourd, and plump the hazel shells
  With a sweet kernel; to set budding more,
And still more, later flowers for the bees,
Until they think warm days will never cease,
    For Summer has o'er-brimmed their clammy
      cells.

Who hath not seen thee oft amid thy store?
  Sometimes whoever seeks abroad may find
  Thee sitting careless on a granary floor,
  Thy hair soft-lifted by a winnowing wind;

Or on a half-reaped furrow sound asleep,
  Drowsed with the fume of poppies, while thy hook
    Spares the next swath and all its twinèd flowers;
And sometimes like a gleaner thou dost keep
  Steady thy laden head across a brook;
  Or by a cider-press, with patient look,
    Thou watchest the last oozings hours by hours.

Where are the songs of Spring? Ay, where are
    they?
  Think not of them, thou hast thy music, too,
While barrèd clouds bloom the soft-dying day,
  And touch the stubble-plains with rosy hue;
Then in a wailful choir the small gnats mourn
  Among the river shallows, borne aloft
    Or sinking as the light wind lives or dies;
And full-grown lambs loud bleat from hilly bourn;
  Hedge-crickets sing; and now with treble soft
  The redbreast whistles from a garden-croft;
    And gathering swallows twitter in the skies.

THE EVE OF ST. AGNES

ST. AGNES' EVE—ah, bitter chill it was!
The owl, for all his feathers, was a-cold;
The hare limped trembling through the frozen grass,
And silent was the flock in woolly fold:
Numb were the Beadsman's fingers while he told
His rosary, and while his frosted breath,
Like pious incense from a censer old,
Seemed taking flight for heaven without a death,
Past the sweet Virgin's picture, while his prayer he
    saith.

His prayer he saith, this patient, holy man;
Then takes his lamp, and riseth from his knees,
And back returneth, meagre, barefoot, wan,
Along the chapel aisle by slow degrees;
The sculptured dead, on each side, seemed to freeze,
Imprisoned in black, purgatorial rails;
Knights, ladies, praying in dumb orat'ries,
He passeth by; and his weak spirit fails
To think how they may ache in icy hoods and mails.

Northward he turneth through a little door,
And scarce three steps, ere Music's golden tongue
Flattered to tears this aged man and poor;
But no—already had his death-bell rung;
The joys of all his life were said and sung;
His was harsh penance on St. Agnes' Eve;
Another way he went, and soon among
Rough ashes sat he for his soul's reprieve,
And all night kept awake, for sinner's sake to grieve.

That ancient Beadsman heard the prelude soft:
And so it chanced, for many a door was wide,
From hurry to and fro. Soon, up aloft,
The silver, snarling trumpets 'gan to chide;
The level chambers, ready with their pride,
Were glowing to receive a thousand guests;
The carvèd angels, ever eager-eyed,
Stared, where upon their heads the cornice rests,
With hair blown back, and wings put crosswise on
        their breasts.

At length burst in the argent revelry,
With plume, tiara, and all rich array,
Numerous as shadows haunting faerily

The brain, new-stuffed, in youth, with triumphs gay
Of old romance. These let us wish away;
And turn, sole-thoughted, to one lady there,
Whose heart had brooded, all that wintry day,
On love, and winged St. Agnes' saintly care,
As she had heard old dames full many times declare.

They told her how, upon St. Agnes' Eve,
Young virgins might have visions of delight,
And soft adorings from their loves receive
Upon the honeyed middle of the night,
If ceremonies due they did aright;
As, supperless to bed they must retire,
And couch supine their beauties, lily white;
Nor look behind, nor sideways, but require
Of Heaven with upward eyes for all that they desire.

Full of this whim was thoughtful Madeline;
The music, yearning like a God in pain,
She scarcely heard; her maiden eyes divine,
Fixed on the floor, saw many a sweeping train
Pass by—she heeded not at all; in vain
Came many a tiptoe, amorous cavalier,
And back retired, not cooled by high disdain,
But she saw not; her heart was otherwhere;
She sighed for Agnes' dreams, the sweetest of the year.

She danced along with vague, regardless eyes,
Anxious her lips, her breathing quick and short;
The hallowed hour was near at hand; she sighs
Amid the timbrels, and the thronged resort
Of whisperers in anger, or in sport;
Mid looks of love, defiance, hate and scorn,

Hoodwinked with fairy fancy; all amort
Save to St. Agnes and her lambs unshorn,
And all the bliss to be before to-morrow morn.

So, purposing each moment to retire,
She lingered still. Meantime, across the moors,
Had come young Porphyro, with heart on fire
For Madeline. Beside the portal doors,
Buttressed from moonlight, stands he, and implores
All saints to give him sight of Madeline;
But for one moment in the tedious hours,
That he might gaze and worship all unseen;
Perchance speak, kneel, touch, kiss—in sooth such
        things have been.

He ventures in; let no buzzed whisper tell;
All eyes be muffled, or a hundred swords
Will storm his heart, love's feverous citadel;
For him, those chambers held barbarian hordes,
Hyena foeman, and hot-blooded lords,
Whose very dogs would execrations howl
Against his lineage; not one breast affords
Him any mercy, in that mansion foul,
Save one old beldame, weak in body and in soul.

Ah, happy chance! the aged creature came,
Shuffling along with ivory-headed wand,
To where he stood, hid from the torch's flame,
Behind a broad hall-pillar, far beyond
The sound of merriment and chorus bland.
He startled her; but soon she knew his face,
And grasped his fingers in her palsied hand,

Saying, "Mercy, Porphyro! hie thee from this place:
They are all here to-night, the whole bloodthirsty
  race!

"Get hence! get hence! there's a dwarfish Hildebrand;
He had a fever late, and in the fit
He cursèd thee and thine, both house and land,
Then there's that old Lord Maurice, not a whit
More tame for his gray hairs—alas me! flit!
Flit like a ghost away!"—"Ah, gossip dear,
We're safe enough; here in this arm-chair sit,
And tell me how—" "Good saints, not here, not here;
Follow me, child, or else these stones will be thy bier."

He followed through a lowly archèd way,
Brushing the cobwebs with his lofty plume:
And as she muttered "Well-a—well-a-day!"
He found him in a little moonlight room,
Pale, latticed, chill, and silent as a tomb.
"Now tell me where is Madeline," said he;
"O, tell me, Angela, by the holy loom
Which none but secret sisterhood may see,
When they St. Agnes' wool are weaving piously."

"St. Agnes! Ah! it is St. Agnes' Eve,
Yet men will murder upon holy days:
Thou must hold water in a witch's sieve,
And be liege-lord of all the elves and fays,
To venture so. It fills me with amaze
To see thee, Porphyro!—St. Agnes' Eve!
God's help! my lady fair the conjurer plays
This very night; good angels her deceive!
But let me laugh awhile, I've mickle time to grieve."

JOHN KEATS

Feebly she laugheth in the languid moon,
While Porphyro upon her face doth look,
Like puzzled urchin on an agèd crone
Who keepeth closed a wondrous riddle-book,
As spectacled she sits in chimney nook.
But soon his eyes grew brilliant, when she told
His lady's purpose; and he scarce could brook
Tears, at the thought of those enchantments cold,
And Madeline asleep in lap of legends old.

Sudden a thought came like a full-blown rose,
Flushing his brow, and in his painèd heart
Made purple riot; then doth he propose
A stratagem that makes the beldame start;
"A cruel man and impious thou art!
Sweet lady, let her pray, and sleep and dream
Alone with her good angels, far apart
From wicked men like thee. Go, go! I deem
Thou canst not surely be the same that thou didst
        seem."

"I will not harm her, by all saints I swear!"
Quoth Porphyro; "O, may I ne'er find grace
When my weak voice shall whisper its last
        prayer,
If one of her soft ringlets I displace,
Or look with ruffian passion in her face:
Good Angela, believe me by these tears;
Or I will, even in a moment's space,
Awake, with horrid shout, my foemen's ears,
And beard them, though they be more fanged than
        wolves and bears."

"Ah! why wilt thou affright a feeble soul?
A poor, weak, palsy-stricken, churchyard thing,
Whose passing-bell may ere the midnight toll;
Whose prayers for thee, each morn and evening,
Were never missed." Thus plaining, doth she bring
A gentler speech from burning Porphyro;
So woful, and of such deep sorrowing,
That Angela gives promise she will do
Whatever he shall wish, betide her weal or woe.

Which was, to lead him, in close secrecy,
Even to Madeline's chamber, and there hide
Him in a closet, of such privacy
That he might see her beauty unespied,
And win perhaps that night a peerless bride;
While legioned fairies paced the coverlet,
And pale enchantment held her sleepy-eyed.
Never on such a night have lovers met,
Since Merlin paid his Demon all the monstrous debt.

"It shall be as thou wishest," said the dame;
"All cates and dainties shall be storèd there
Quickly on this feast-night; by the tambour frame
Her own lute thou wilt see; no time to spare,
For I am slow and feeble, and scarce dare
On such a catering trust my dizzy head.
Wait here, my child, with patience kneel in prayer
The while. Ah! thou must needs the lady wed,
Or may I never leave my grave among the dead."

So saying, she hobbled off with busy fear.
The lover's endless minutes slowly passed:
The dame returned, and whispered in his ear
To follow her; with aged eyes aghast

From fright of dim espial. Safe at last,
Through many a dusky gallery, they gain
The maiden's chamber, silken, hushed and chaste;
Where Porphyro took covert, pleased amain.
His poor guide hurried back with agues in her
    brain.

Her faltering hand upon the balustrade,
Old Angela was feeling for the stair,
When Madeline, St. Agnes' charmèd maid,
Rose, like a missioned spirit, unaware;
With silver taper's light, and pious care,
She turned, and down the agèd gossip led
To a safe level matting. Now prepare
Young Porphyro, for gazing on that bed!
She comes, she comes again, like a ring-dove frayed
    and fled.

Out went the taper as she hurried in;
Its little smoke, in pallid moonshine, died;
She closed the door, she panted, all akin
To spirits of the air, and visions wide;
No uttered syllable, or, woe betide!
But to her heart, her heart was voluble,
Paining with eloquence her balmy side;
As though a tongueless nightingale should swell
Her throat in vain, and die, heart-stifled in her
    dell.

A casement high and triple-arched there was,
All garlanded with carven imageries
Of fruits, and flowers, and bunches of knot-grass,
And diamonded with panes of quaint device,

Innumerable of stains and splendid dyes,
As are the tiger-moth's deep-damasked wings;
And in the midst, 'mong thousand heraldries,
And twilight saints, and dim emblazonings,
A shielded scutcheon blushed with blood of queens
      and kings.

Full on this casement shone the wintry moon,
And threw warm gules on Madeline's fair breast,
As down she knelt for Heaven's grace and boon:
Rose-bloom fell on her hands, together prest,
And on her silver cross soft amethyst,
And on her hair a glory, like a saint;
She seemed a splendid angel, newly drest,
Save wings, for Heaven. Porphyro grew faint:
She knelt, so pure a thing, so free from mortal
      taint.

Anon his heart revives; her vespers done,
Of all its wreathèd pearls her hair she frees;
Unclasps her warmèd jewels one by one;
Loosens her fragrant bodice; by degrees
Her rich attire creeps rustling to her knees.
Half hidden, like a mermaid in sea-weed,
Pensive awhile she dreams awake, and sees,
In fancy, fair St. Agnes in her bed,
But dares not look behind, or all the charm is fled.

Soon, trembling in her soft and chilly nest,
In sort of wakeful swoon, perplexed she lay,
Until the poppied warmth of sleep oppressed
Her soothèd limbs, and soul fatigued away;
Flown like a thought, until the morrow-day;

JOHN KEATS

Blissfully havened both from joy and pain;
Clasped like a missal where swart Paynims pray;
Blinded alike from sunshine and from rain,
As though a rose should shut, and be a bud again.

Stolen to this paradise, and so entranced,
Porphyro gazed upon her empty dress,
And listened to her breathing, if it chanced
To wake into a slumberous tenderness;
Which when he heard, that minute did he bless,
And breathed himself; then from the closet crept,
Noiseless as fear in a wide wilderness,
And over the hushed carpet, silent, stept,
And 'tween the curtains peeped, and where, lo!—
        how fast she slept.

Then by the bedside, where the faded moon
Made a dim, silver twilight, soft he set
A table, and, half anguished, threw thereon
A cloth of woven crimson, gold and jet.
O for some drowsy Morphean amulet!
The boisterous, midnight, festive clarion,
The kettle-drum, and far-heard clarionet,
Affray his ears, though but in dying tone:
The hall-door shuts again, and all the noise is gone.

And still she slept an azure-lidded sleep,
In blanchèd linen, smooth and lavendered;
While he from forth the closet brought a heap
Of candied apple, quince and plum and gourd,
With jellies soother than the creamy curd,
And lucent syrops, tinct with cinnamon;
Manna and dates, in argosy transferred

From Fez; and spicèd dainties, every one,
From silken Samarcand to cedared Lebanon.

These delicates he heaped with glowing hand
On golden dishes and in baskets bright
Of wreathèd silver. Sumptuous they stand
In the retired quiet of the night,
Filling the chilly room with perfume light.
"And now, my love, my seraph fair, awake!
Thou art my heaven, and I thine eremite;
Open thine eyes, for meek St. Agnes' sake,
Or I shall drowse beside thee, so my soul doth
    ache."

Thus whispering, his warm, unnervèd arm
Sank in her pillow. Shaded was her dream
By the dusk curtains: 'twas a midnight charm
Impossible to melt as icèd stream:
The lustrous salvers in the moonlight gleam
Broad golden fringe upon the carpet lies:
It seemed he never, never could redeem
From such a steadfast spell his lady's eyes;
So mused awhile, entoiled in woofèd fantasies.

Awakening up, he took her hollow lute,
Tumultuous, and, in chords that tenderest be,
He played an ancient ditty, long since mute,
In Provence called "La belle Dame sans merci,"
Close to her ear touching the melody—
Wherewith disturbed, she uttered a soft moan;
He ceased—she panted quick—and suddenly
Her blue affrayèd eyes wide open shone;
Upon his knees he sank, pale as smooth-sculptured
    stone.

Her eyes were open, but she still beheld,
Now wide awake, the vision of her sleep.
There was a painful change, that nigh expelled
The blisses of her dream so pure and deep;
At which fair Madeline began to weep,
And moan forth witless words with many a sigh;
While still her gaze on Porphyro would keep.
Who knelt, with joinèd hands and piteous eye,
Fearing to move or speak, she looked so dreamingly.

"Ah, Porphyro!" said she, "but even now
Thy voice was at sweet tremble in mine ear,
Made tunable with every sweetest vow;
And those sad eyes were spiritual and clear.
How changed thou art! how pallid, chill and drear!
Give me that voice again, my Porphyro,
Those looks immortal, those complainings dear!
O, leave me not in this eternal woe,
For if thou diest, my Love, I know not where to
        go."

Beyond a mortal man impassioned far
At these voluptuous accents, he arose,
Ethereal, flushed, and like a throbbing star
Seen mid the sapphire Heaven's deep repose:
Into her dream he melted, as the rose
Blendeth its odor with the violet—
Solution sweet: meantime the frost-wind blows
Like love's alarum pattering the sharp sleet
Against the window-panes; St. Agnes' moon hath set.

'Tis dark; quick pattereth the flaw-blown sleet;
"This is no dream, my bride, my Madeline!"

'Tis dark; the icèd gusts still rave and beat:
"No dream, alas! alas! and woe is mine!
Porphyro will leave me here to fade and pine.
Cruel! what traitor could thee hither bring?
I curse not, for my heart is lost in thine,
Though thou forsakest a deceivèd thing—
A dove forlorn and lost, with sick, unprunèd wing."

"My Madeline! sweet dreamer! lovely bride!
Say, may I be for aye thy vassal blest?
Thy beauty's shield, heart-shaped and vermeil dyed?
Ah, silver shrine, here will I take my rest
After so many hours of toil and quest,
A famished pilgrim saved by miracle.
Though I have found, I will not rob thy nest,
Saving of thy sweet self; if thou think'st well
To trust, fair Madeline, to no rude infidel.

"Hark! 't is an elfin-storm from faery land,
Of haggard seeming, but a boon indeed:
Arise—arise! the morning is at hand—
The bloated wassaillers will never heed:—
Let us away, my love, with happy speed;
There are no ears to hear, or eyes to see—
Drowned all in Rhenish and the sleepy mead:
Awake! arise! my love, and fearless be,
For o'er the southern moors I have a home for thee."

She hurried at his words, beset with fears.
For there were sleeping dragons all around,
At glaring watch, perhaps, with ready spears—
Down the wide stairs with a darkling way they
found.

In all the house was heard no human sound.
A chain-drooped lamp was flickering by each door;
The arras, rich with horseman, hawk and hound,
Fluttered in the besieging wind's uproar;
And the long carpets rose along the gusty floor.

They glide, like phantoms, into the wide hall!
Like phantoms to the iron porch they glide,
Where lay the porter, in uneasy sprawl,
With a huge empty flagon by his side.
The wakeful bloodhound rose, and shook his hide,
But his sagacious eye an inmate owns;
By one, and one, the bolts full easy slide;
The chains lie silent on the footworn stones;
The key turns, and the door upon its hinges groans.

And they are gone! ay, ages long ago
These lovers fled away into the storm.
That night the baron dreamt of many a woe,
And all his warrior-guests, with shade and form
Of witch, and demon, and large coffin-worm,
Were long be-nightmared. Angela the old
Died palsy-twitched, with meagre face deform;
The beadsman, after thousand aves told,
For aye unsought-for slept among his ashes cold.

HARRY KEMP
1883—

THANKS

I KNEEL not now to pray that Thou
    Make white one single sin,
I only kneel to thank thee, Lord,
    For what I have not been—

For deeds which sprouted in my heart
    But ne'er to bloom were brought,
For monstrous vices which I slew
    In the shambles of my thought—

Dark seeds the world has never guessed,
    By hell and passion bred,
Which never grew beyond the bud
    That cankered in my head.

Some said I was a righteous man—
    Poor fools! The gallows tree
(If thou hadst let one foot to slip)
    Had grown a limb for me.

THE CONQUERORS

I saw the Conquerors riding by
    With trampling feet of horse and men:
Empire on empire like the tide
    Flooded the world and ebbed again.

A thousand banners caught the sun,
    And cities smoked along the plain
And laden down with silk and gold
    And heaped-up pillage groaned the wain.

I saw the Conquerors riding by,
    Splashing through loathsome floods of war—
The Crescent leaning o'er its hosts,
    And the barbaric scimitar—

And continents of moving spears,
    And storms of arrows in the sky,

And all the instruments sought out
  By cunning men that men may die!

I saw the Conquerors riding by
  With cruel lips and faces wan:
Musing on kingdoms sacked and burned
  There rode the Mongol Genghis Khan;

And Alexander, like a god,
  Who sought to weld the world in one;
And Cæsar with his laurel wreath;
  And like a thing from Hell, the Hun;

And leading, like a star the van,
  Heedless of upstretched arm and groan,
Inscrutable Napoleon went
  Dreaming of empire, and alone . . .

Then all they perished from the earth
  As fleeting shadows from a glass,
And, conquering down the centuries,
  Came Christ, the Swordless, on an ass!

THEDA KENYON
HEREDITY

THERE is a Pirate in my blood,
  And a rare, great Queen:
And all that the one has understood,
  The other has never seen.

At noon, I tread on cloth o' gold,—
  And the Pirate watches me;
His hand is light in a rapier hold,
  And he hungers for the sea!

At night, the wind is in my hair,
   And I own the sea to the sky—
But the Queen's lips twist, as she watches there,
   And she shudders as I go by.

My arrogant head knows the weight of a crown—
   But a quarterdeck sired my stride.
There's a regal form in my velvet gown—
   But my heart keeps time to the tide!

There is a Pirate deep in me—
   But his crew-command seems small;
There is a Queen—and she cannot see
   Why she frets at a palace wall!

CAROLINE KEPPEL

1735—

ROBIN ADAIR

WHAT's this dull town to me?
    Robin's not near,
He whom I wished to see,
    Wished for to hear;
Where's all the joy and mirth
Made life a heaven on earth,
Oh, they're all fled with thee,
    Robin Adair!

What made the assembly shine?
    Robin Adair:
What made the ball so fine?
    Robin was there:

CAROLINE KEPPEL

What, when the play was o'er,
What made my heart so sore?
Oh, it was parting with
 Robin Adair!

But now thou art far from me,
 Robin Adair;
But now I never see
 Robin Adair;
Yet him I loved so well
Still in my heart shall dwell:
Oh, I can ne'er forget
 Robin Adair!

Welcome on shore again,
 Robin Adair!
Welcome once more again,
 Robin Adair!
I feel thy trembling hand:
Tears in thy eyelids stand,
To greet thy native land,
 Robin Adair.

Long I ne'er saw thee, Love,
 Robin Adair;
Still I prayed for thee, Love,
 Robin Adair:
When thou wert far at sea,
Many made love to me,
But still I thought on thee,
 Robin Adair.

Come to my heart again,
　　Robin Adair;
Never to part again,
　　Robin Adair;
And if thou still art true,
I will be constant too,
And will wed none but you,
　　Robin Adair!

FRANCIS SCOTT KEY
1780—1843.
THE STAR-SPANGLED BANNER

O SAY, can you see, by the dawn's early light,
　What so proudly we hailed at the twilight's last
　　gleaming—
Whose broad stripes and bright stars, through the
　clouds of the fight,
　O'er the ramparts we watched were so gallantly
　　streaming!
And the rocket's red glare, the bombs bursting in
　air,
Gave proof through the night that our flag was
　still there;
O! say, does that star-spangled banner yet wave
O'er the land of the free, and the home of the
　brave?

On that shore dimly seen through the mists of the
　deep,
　Where the foe's haughty host in dread silence
　　reposes,

What is that which the breeze, o'er the towering
   steep,
  As it fitfully blows, now conceals, now discloses?
Now it catches the gleam of the morning's first
   beam,
In full glory reflected now shines on the stream;
'T is the star-spangled banner; O long may it wave
O'er the land of the free, and the home of the
   brave!

And where is that band who so vauntingly swore
  That the havoc of war and the battle's confusion
A home and a country should leave us no more?
  Their blood has washed out their foul footsteps'
   pollution.
No refuge could save the hireling and slave
From the terror of flight, or the gloom of the grave;
And the star-spangled banner in triumph doth wave
O'er the land of the free, and the home of the
   brave.

O! thus be it ever, when freemen shall stand
  Between their loved homes and the war's desola-
   tion!
Blest with victory and peace, may the heav'en-res-
   cued land
  Praise the power that hath made and preserved
   us a nation.
Then conquer we must, when our cause it is just,
And this be our motto—"*In God is our trust:*"
And the star-spangled banner in triumph shall wave
O'er the land of the free, and the home of the
   brave.

OMAR KHAYYÁM
1025—1123
PERSIAN
Translated by Edward Fitzgerald
1809—1883

THE RUBÁIYÁT OF OMAR KHAYYÁM

I.

WAKE? For the Sun, who scatter'd into flight
The Stars before him from the Field of Night,
   Drives Night along with them from Heav'n, and strikes
The Sultán's Turret with a Shaft of Light.

II.

Before the phantom of False morning died,
Methought a Voice within the Tavern cried,
   "When all the Temple is prepared within,
"Why nods the drowsy Worshipper outside?"

III.

And, as the Cock crew, those who stood before
The Tavern shouted—"Open then the Door!
   "You know how little while we have to stay,
"And, once departed, may return no more."

IV.

Now the New Year reviving old Desires,
The thoughtful Soul to Solitude retires,
   Where the WHITE HAND OF MOSES on the Bough,
Puts out, and Jesus from the Ground suspires.

OMAR KHAYYÁM

V.

Iram indeed is gone with all his Rose,
And Jamshyd's Sev'n-ring'd Cup where no one
    knows;
  But still a Ruby kindles in the Vine,
And many a Garden by the Water blows.

VI.

And David's lips are lockt; but in divine
High-piping, Pehleví, with "Wine! Wine! Wine!
  "Red Wine!"—the Nightingale cries to the Rose
That sallow cheek of hers to' incarnadine.

VII.

Come, fill the Cup, and in the fire of Spring
Your Winter-garment of Repentance fling:
  The Bird of Time has but a little way
To flutter—and the Bird is on the Wing.

VIII.

Whether at Naishápúr or Babylon,
Whether the Cup with sweet or bitter run,
  The Wine of Life keeps oozing drop by drop,
The Leaves of Life keep falling one by one.

IX.

Each Morn a thousand Roses brings, you say:
Yes, but where leaves the Rose of Yesterday?
  And this first Summer month that brings the
    Rose
Shall take Jamshyd and Kaikobád away.

X.

Well, let it take them! What have we to do
With Kaikobád the Great, or Kaikhosrú?
Let Zál and Rustum bluster as they will,
Or Hátim call to Supper—heed not you.

XI.

With me along the strip of Herbage strown
That just divides the desert from the sown,
Where name of Slave and Sultán is forgot—
And Peace to Mahmúd on his golden Throne!

XII.

A Book of Verses underneath the Bough,
A Jug of Wine, a Loaf of Bread—and Thou
Beside me singing in the Wilderness—
Oh, Wilderness were Paradise enow!

XIII.

Some for the Glories of This World; and some
Sigh for the Prophet's Paradise to come;
Ah, take the Cash, and let the Credit go,
Nor heed the rumble of a distant Drum!

XIV.

Look to the blowing Rose about us—"Lo,
"Laughing," she says, "into the world I blow,
"At once the silken tassel of my Purse
"Tear, and its Treasure on the Garden throw."

XV.

And those who husbanded the Golden grain,
And those who flung it to the winds like Rain,

Alike to no such aureat Earth are turn'd
As, buried once, Men want dug up again.

XVI.

The Worldly Hope men set their Hearts upon
Turns Ashes—or it prospers; and anon,
   Like Snow upon the Desert's dusty Face,
Lighting a little hour or two—is gone.

XVII.

Think, in this batter'd Caravanserai
Whose Portals are alternate Night and Day,
   How Sultán after Sultán with his Pomp
Abode his destined Hour, and went his way.

XVIII.

They say the Lion and the Lizard keep
The Courts where Jamshyd gloried and drank deep:
   And Bahrám, that great Hunter—the Wild Ass
Stamps o'er his Head, but cannot break his Sleep.

XIX.

I sometimes think that never blows so red
The Rose as where some buried Cæsar bled;
   That every Hyacinth the Garden wears
Dropt in her Lap from some once lovely Head.

XX.

And this reviving Herb whose tender Green
Fledges the River-Lip on which we lean—
   Ah, lean upon it lightly! for who knows
From what once lovely Lip it springs unseen!

XXI.

Ah, my Belovéd, fill the Cup that clears
TO-DAY of past Regrets and future Fears:
    To-morrow!—Why, To-morrow I may be
Myself with Yesterday's Sev'n Thousand Years.

XXII.

For some we loved, the loveliest and the best
That from his Vintage rolling Time hath prest,
    Have drunk their Cup a Round or two before,
And one by one crept silently to rest.

XXIII.

And we, that now make merry in the Room
They left, and Summer dresses in new bloom,
    Ourselves must we beneath the Couch of Earth
Descend—ourselves to make a Couch—for whom?

XXIV.

Ah, make the most of what we yet may spend,
Before we too into the Dust descend;
    Dust into Dust, and under Dust to lie,
Sans Wine, sans Song, sans Singer, and—sans End!

XXV.

Alike for those who for TO-DAY prepare,
And those that after some TO-MORROW stare,
    A Muezzín from the Tower of Darkness cries,
"Fools! your Reward is neither Here nor There."

XXVI.

Why, all the Saints and Sages who discuss'd
Of the Two Worlds so wisely—they are thrust

OMAR KHAYYÁM

Like foolish Prophets forth; their Words to Scorn
Are scatter'd, and their Mouths are stopt with Dust.

XXVII.

Myself when young did eagerly frequent
Doctor and Saint, and heard great argument
   About it and about: but evermore
Came out by the same door where in I went.

XXVIII.

With them the seed of Wisdom did I sow,
And with mine own hand wrought to make it grow;
   And this was all the Harvest that I reap'd—
"I came like Water, and like Wind I go."

XXIX.

Into this Universe, and *Why* not knowing
Nor *Whence*, like Water willy-nilly flowing;
   And out of it, as Wind along the Waste,
I know not *Whither*, willy-nilly blowing.

XXX.

What, without asking, hither hurried *Whence*?
And, without asking, *Whither* hurried hence!
   Oh, many a Cup of this forbidden Wine
Must drown the memory of that insolence!

XXXI.

Up from Earth's Centre through the Seventh Gate
I rose, and on the Throne of Saturn sate,
   And many a Knot unravel'd by the Road;
But not the Master-knot of Human Fate.

XXXII.

There was the Door to which I found no Key;
There was the Veil through which I might not see:
   Some little talk awhile of ME and THEE
There was—and then no more of THEE and ME.

XXXIII.

Earth could not answer; nor the Seas that mourn
In flowing Purple, of their Lord forlorn;
   Nor rolling Heaven, with all his Signs reveal'd
And hidden by the sleeve of Night and Morn.

XXXIV.

Then of the THEE IN ME who works behind
The Veil, I lifted up my hands to find
   A lamp amid the Darkness; and I heard,
As from Without—"THE ME WITHIN THEE BLIND!"

XXXV.

Then to the Lip of this poor earthen Urn
I lean'd, the Secret of my Life to learn:
   And Lip to Lip it murmur'd—"While you live,
"Drink!—for, once dead, you never shall return."

XXXVI.

I think the Vessel, that with fugitive
Articulation answer'd, once did live,
   And drink; and Ah! the passive Lip I kiss'd,
How many Kisses might it take—and give!

XXXVII.

For I remember stopping by the way
To watch a Potter thumping his wet Clay:

And with its all-obliterated Tongue
It murmur'd—"Gently, Brother, gently, pray!"

XXXVIII.

And has not such a Story from of Old
Down Man's successive generations roll'd
   Of such a clod of saturated Earth
Cast by the Maker into Human mould?

XXXIX.

And not a drop that from our Cups we throw
For Earth to drink of, but may steal below
   To quench the fire of Anguish in some Eye
There hidden—far beneath, and long ago.

XL.

As then the Tulip for her morning sup
Of Heav'nly Vintage from the soil looks up,
   Do you devoutly do the like, till Heav'n
To Earth invert you—like an empty Cup.

XLI.

Perplex no more with Human or Divine,
To-morrow's tangle to the winds resign,
   And lose your fingers in the tresses of
The Cypress-slender Minister of Wine.

XLII.

And if the Wine you drink, the Lip you press,
End in what All begins and ends in—Yes;
   Think then you are TO-DAY what YESTERDAY
You were—TO-MORROW you shall not be less.

XLIII.

So when that Angel of the darker Drink
At last shall find you by the river-brink,
   And, offering his Cup, invite your Soul
Forth to your Lips to quaff—you shall not shrink.

XLIV.

Why, if the Soul can fling the Dust aside,
And naked on the Air of Heaven ride,
   Were't not a Shame—were't not a Shame for him
In this clay carcase crippled to abide?

XLV.

'Tis but a Tent where takes his one day's rest
A Sultán to the realm of Death addrest;
   The Sultán rises, and the dark Ferrásh
Strikes, and prepares it for another Guest.

XLVI.

And fear not lest Existence closing your
Account, and mine, should know the like no more;
   The Eternal Sákí from that Bowl has pour'd
Millions of Bubbles like us, and will pour.

XLVII.

When You and I behind the Veil are past,
Oh, but the long, long while the World shall last,
   Which of our Coming and Departure heeds
As the Sea's self should heed a pebble-cast.

XLVIII.

A Moment's Halt—a momentary taste
Of Being from the Well amid the Waste—

And Lo!—the phantom Caravan has reach'd
The NOTHING it set out from—Oh, make haste!

XLIX.

Would you that spangle of Existence spend
About THE SECRET—quick about it, Friend!
    A Hair perhaps divides the False and True—
And upon what, prithee, may life depend?

L.

A Hair perhaps divides the False and True;
Yes; and a single Alif were the clue—
    Could you but find it—to the Treasure-house,
And peradventure to THE MASTER too;

LI.

Whose secret Presence, through Creation's veins
Running Quicksilver-like eludes your pains;
    Taking all shapes from Máh to Máhi; and
They change and perish all—but He remains;

LII.

A moment guess'd—then back behind the Fold
Immerst of Darkness round the Drama roll'd
    Which, for the Pastime of Eternity,
He doth Himself contrive, enact, behold.

LIII.

But if in vain, down on the stubborn floor
Of Earth, and up to Heav'n's unopening Door,
    You gaze TO-DAY, while You and You—how
        then
TO-MORROW, when You shall be You no more?

LIV.

Waste not your Hour, nor in the vain pursuit
Of This and That endeavour and dispute;
   Better be jocund with the fruitful Grape
Than sadden after none, or bitter, Fruit.

LV.

You know, my Friends, with what a brave Carouse
I made a Second Marriage in my house;
   Divorced old barren Reason from my Bed,
And took the Daughter of the Vine to Spouse.

LVI.

For "Is" and "Is-NOT" though with Rule and Line
And "UP-AND-DOWN" by Logic I define,
   Of all that one should care to fathom, I
Was never deep in anything but—Wine.

LVII.

Ah, but my Computations, People say,
Reduced the Year to better reckoning?—Nay,
   'Twas only striking from the Calendar
Unborn To-morrow and dead Yesterday.

LVIII.

And lately, by the Tavern Door agape,
Came shining through the Dusk an Angel Shape
   Bearing a Vessel on his Shoulder; and
He bid me taste of it; and 'twas—the Grape!

LIX.

The Grape that can with Logic absolute
The Two-and-Seventy jarring Sects confute:

OMAR KHAYYÁM

The sovereign Alchemist that in a trice
Life's leaden metal into Gold transmute:

LX.

The mighty Mahmúd, Allah-breathing Lord,
That all the misbelieving and black Horde
    Of Fears and Sorrows that infest the Soul
Scatters before him with his whirlwind Sword.

LXI.

Why, be this Juice the growth of God, who dare
Blaspheme the twisted tendril as a Snare?
    A Blessing, we should use it, should we not?
And if a Curse—why, then, Who set it there?

LXII.

I must abjure the Balm of Life, I must,
Scared by some After-reckoning ta'en on trust,
    Or lured with Hope of some Diviner Drink,
To fill the Cup—when crumbled into Dust!

LXIII.

Oh threats of Hell and Hopes of Paradise!
One thing at least is certain—*This* Life flies:
    One thing is certain and the rest is Lies;
The Flower that once has blown for ever dies.

LXIV.

Strange, is it not? that of the myriads who
Before us pass'd the door of Darkness through,
    Not one returns to tell us of the Road,
Which to discover we must travel too.

LXV.

The Revelations of Devout and Learn'd
Who rose before us, and as Prophets burn'd,
  Are all but Stories, which, awoke from Sleep
They told their comrades, and to Sleep return'd.

LXVI.

I sent my Soul through the Invisible,
Some letter of that After-life to spell:
  And by and by my Soul return'd to me,
And answer'd "I Myself am Heav'n and Hell:"

LXVII.

Heav'n but the Vision of fulfill'd Desire,
And Hell the Shadow from a Soul on fire,
  Cast on the Darkness into which Ourselves,
So late emerged from, shall so soon expire.

LXVIII.

We are no other than a moving row
Of Magic Shadow-shapes that come and go
  Round with the Sun-illumined Lantern held
In Midnight by the Master of the Show;

LXIX.

But helpless Pieces of the Game He plays
Upon this Checquer-board of Nights and Days;
  Hither and thither moves, and checks, and slays,
And one by one back in the Closet lays.

LXX.

The Ball no question makes of Ayes and Nayes,
But Here or There as strikes the Player goes;

And He that toss'd you down into the Field,
He knows about it all—HE knows—HE knows!

LXXI.

The Moving Finger writes; and, having writ,
Moves on: nor all your Piety nor Wit
 Shall lure it back to cancel half a Line,
Nor all your Tears wash out a Word of it.

LXXII.

And that inverted Bowl they call the Sky,
Whereunder crawling coop'd we live and die,
 Lift not your hands to *It* for help—for It
As impotently moves as you or I.

LXXIII.

With Earth's first Clay They did the Last Man
  knead,
And there of the Last Harvest sow'd the Seed:
 And the first Morning of Creation wrote
What the Last Dawn of Reckoning shall read.

LXXIV.

YESTERDAY *This* Day's Madness did prepare;
TO-MORROW's Silence, Triumph, or Despair:
 Drink! for you know not whence you came, nor
  why:
Drink! for you know not why you go, nor where.

LXXV.

I tell you this—When, started from the Goal,
Over the flaming shoulders of the Foal

Of Heav'n Parwín and Mushtarí they flung,
In my predestined Plot of Dust and Soul.

LXXVI.

The Vine had struck a fibre: which about
If clings my Being—let the Dervish flout;
　Of my Base metal may be filed a Key
That shall unlock the Door he howls without.

LXXVII.

And this I know: whether the one True Light
Kindle to Love, or Wrath-consume me quite,
　One Flash of It within the Tavern caught
Better than in the Temple lost outright.

LXXVIII.

What! out of senseless Nothing to provoke
A conscious Something to resent the yoke
　Of unpermitted Pleasure, under pain
Of Everlasting Penalites, if broke!

LXXIX.

What! from his helpless Creature be repaid
Pure Gold for what he lent him dross-allay'd—
　Sue for a Debt he never did contract,
And cannot answer—Oh the sorry trade!

LXXX.

Oh Thou, who didst with pitfall and with gin
Beset the Road I was to wander in,
　Thou wilt not with Predestined Evil round
Enmesh, and then impute my Fall to Sin!

OMAR KHAYYÁM

LXXXI.

Oh Thou, who Man of baser Earth didst make,
And ev'n with Paradise devise the Snake:
   For all the Sin wherewith the Face of Man
Is blacken'd—Man's forgiveness give—and take!

*   *   *   *   *   *   *   *

LXXXII.

As under cover of departing Day
Slunk hunger-stricken Ramazán away,
   Once more within the Potter's house alone
I stood, surrounded by the Shapes of Clay.

LXXXIII.

Shapes of all Sorts and Sizes, great and small,
That stood along the floor and by the wall;
   And some loquacious Vessels were; and some
Listen'd perhaps, but never talk'd at all.

LXXXIV.

Said one among them—"Surely not in vain
"My substance of the common Earth was ta'en
   "And to this Figure moulded, to be broke,
"Or trampled back to shapeless Earth again."

LXXXV.

Then said a Second—"Ne'er a peevish Boy
"Would break the Bowl from which he drank in
     joy;
   "And He that with his hand the Vessel made
"Will surely not in after Wrath destroy."

LXXXVI.

After a momentary silence spake
Some Vessel of a more ungainly Make;
  "They sneer at me for leaning all awry:
"What! did the Hand then of the Potter shake?"

LXXXVII.

Whereat some one of the loquacious Lot—
I think a Súfi pipkin—waxing hot—
  "All this of Pot and Potter—Tell me, then,
"Who is the Potter, pray, and who the Pot?"

LXXXVIII.

"Why," said another, "Some there are who tell
"Of one who threatens he will toss to Hell
  "The luckless Pots he marr'd in making—Pish!
"He's a Good Fellow, and 'twill all be well."

LXXXIX.

"Well," murmur'd one, "Let whoso make or buy,
"My Clay with long Oblivion is gone dry:
  "But fill me with the old familiar Juice,
"Methinks I might recover by and by."

XC.

So while the Vessels one by one were speaking,
The little Moon look'd in that all were seeking:
  And then they jogg'd each other, "Brother!
    Brother!
"Now for the Porter's shoulder-knot a-creaking!"

*   *   *   *   *   *   *   *

XCI.

Ah, with the Grape my fading life provide,
And wash the Body whence the Life has died,
   And lay me, shrouded in the living Leaf,
By some not unfrequented Garden-side.

XCII.

That ev'n my buried Ashes such a snare
Of Vintage shall fling up into the Air
   As not a True-believer passing by
But shall be overtaken unaware.

XCIII.

Indeed the Idols I have loved so long
Have done my credit in this World much wrong:
   Have drown'd my Glory in a shallow Cup,
And sold my Reputation for a Song.

XCIV.

Indeed, indeed, Repentance oft before
I swore—but was I sober when I swore?
   And then and then came Spring, and Rose-in-hand
My thread-bare Penitence apieces tore.

XCV.

And much as Wine has play'd the Infidel,
And robb'd me of my Robe of Honour—Well,
   I wonder often what the Vintners buy
One half so precious as the stuff they sell.

XCVI.

Yet Ah, that Spring should vanish with the Rose!
That Youth's sweet-scented manuscript should close!

The Nightingale that in the branches sang,
Ah whence, and whither flown again, who knows!

XCVII.

Would but the Desert of the Fountain yield
One glimpse—if dimly, yet indeed, reveal'd,
    To which the fainting Traveller might spring,
As springs the trampled herbage of the field!

XCVIII.

Would but some wingéd Angel ere too late
Arrest the yet unfolded Roll of Fate,
    And make the stern Recorder otherwise
Enregister, or quite obliterate!

XCIX.

Ah Love! could you and I with Him conspire
To grasp this sorry Scheme of Things entire,
    Would not we shatter it to bits—and then
Re-mould it nearer to the Heart's Desire!

* * * * * * * * * *

C.

Yon rising Moon that looks for us again—
How oft hereafter will she wax and wane;
    How oft hereafter rising look for us
Through this same Garden—and for *one* in vain?

CI.

And when like her, oh Sákí, you shall pass
Among the Guests Star-scatter'd on the Grass,
    And in your joyous errand reach the spot
Where I made One—turn down an empty Glass!

JOYCE KILMER
1886—1918
TREES

I THINK that I shall never see
A poem lovely as a tree.

A tree whose hungry mouth is prest
Against the earth's sweet flowing breast;

A tree that looks at God all day
And lifts her leafy arms to pray;

A tree that may in summer wear
A nest of robins in her hair;

Upon whose bosom snow has lain;
Who intimately lives with rain.

Poems are made by fools like me,
But only God can make a tree.

BEN KING
1857—1894
THE PESSIMIST

NOTHING to do but work,
  Nothing to eat but food,
Nothing to wear but clothes
  To keep one from going nude.

Nothing to breathe but air
  Quick as a flash 't is gone;
Nowhere to fall but off,
  Nowhere to stand but on.

Nothing to comb but hair,
  Nowhere to sleep but in bed,
Nothing to weep but tears,
  Nothing to bury but dead.

Nothing to sing but songs,
  Ah, well, alas! alack!
Nowhere to go but out,
  Nowhere to come but back.

Nothing to see but sights,
  Nothing to quench but thirst,
Nothing to have but what we've got;
  Thus through life we are cursed.

Nothing to strike but a gait,
  Everything moves that goes;
Nothing at all but common sense
  Can ever withstand these woes.

IF I CAN BE BY HER

I D-D-DON'T C-C-C-are how the r-r-r-obin sings,
Er how the r-r-r-ooster f-f-flaps his wings,
Er whether 't sh-sh-shines, er whether 't pours,
Er how high up the eagle s-s-soars,
  If I can b-b-b-be by her.

I don't care if the p-p-p-people s-say
'At I'm weak-minded every-w-way,
An' n-n-never had no cuh-common sense,
I'd c-c-c-cuh-climb the highest p-picket fence
     If I could b-b-b-be by her.

If I can be by h-h-her, I'll s-s-swim
The r-r-r-est of life thro' th-th-thick an' thin;
I'll throw my overcoat away,
An' s-s-s-stand out on the c-c-c-oldest day,
     If I can b-b-b-be by her.

You s-s-see sh-sh-she weighs an awful pile,
B-b-b-but I d-d-d-don't care—sh-she's just my style,
An' any f-f-fool could p-p-p-lainly see
She'd look well b-b-b-by the side of me,
     If I could b-b-b-be by her.

I b-b-b-braced right up, and had the s-s-s-and
To ask 'er f-f-f-father f-f-fer 'er hand;
He said: "Wh-wh-what p-p-prospects have you
    got?"
I said: "I gu-gu-guess I've got a lot,
     If I can b-b-b-be by her."

It's all arranged f-f-fer Christmas Day,
Fer then we're goin' to r-r-r-run away,
An' then s-s-some th-th-thing that cu-cu-couldn't
    be
At all b-b-efore will then, you s-s-see,
     B-b-b-because I'll b-b-b-be by her.

IF I SHOULD DIE

IF I should die to-night
And you should come to my cold corpse and say,
Weeping and heartsick o'er my lifeless clay—
   If I should die to-night,
And you should come in deepest grief and woe—
And say: "Here's that ten dollars that I owe,"
   I might arise in my large white cravat
   And say, "What's that?"

   If I should die to-night
And you should come to my cold corpse and kneel,
Clasping my bier to show the grief you feel,
   I say, if I should die to-night
And you should come to me, and there and then
Just even hint 'bout payin' me that ten,
   I might arise the while,
   But I'd drop dead again.

THE COW SLIPS AWAY

   THE tall pines pine,
   The pawpaws pause,
And the bumble-bee bumbles all day;
   The eavesdropper drops,
   And the grasshopper hops,
While gently the cow slips away.